MARTIN KYRLE'S

LITTLE BLUE NIGHTBOOK

© Martin Kyrle 2013
2nd Edition 2023

Front cover and illustrations by Derek Snowdon.
By the same author:
Martin Kyrle's Little Green Nightbook
Martin Kyrle's Little Orange Nightbook
Jottings from the Trans-Siberian Railway
Jottings from Russia and the Baltic States. Part 1: Russia and Estonia

The Liberals in Hampshire – a Part(l)y History
   Part 1: Southampton 1958-65: object lessons
   Part 2: Eastleigh 1965-72: out in the suburbs, something stirred!
   Part 3: Eastleigh 1972-81: the thorn in the flesh bursts into flower
   Part 4: Eastleigh 1978-85: a campaign in pictures – politics can be fun!
   Part 5: Eastleigh 1981-90: control!
A 20-20 Vision – turning Britain into a liberal democracy

In preparation:
Jottings from Russia and the Baltic States. Part 2: Latvia, Lithuania and Finland
A Victorian Childhood

Europe and Asia maps sourced from d-maps.com

All rights reserved. No part of this publication may be reproduced, stored in a retrieval system or transmitted in any form or by any means without prior permission of the publishers.

ISBN 978-0-9564701-6-4

Printed by Sarsen Press

CONTENTS

                                        page

Preface v
Introduction 1
A   *In at the beginning* 5
B   *A Window on the East*
     (with acknowledgements to Peter the Great) 17
C   *'...to Caunterbury they wende' (Chaucer)* 29
D   *... and Plan A* 43
E   *'Tis an ill clutch that blows nobody any good...* 49
F   *Returning to normal* 57
G   *Stone me!* 65
H   *'The Good Old Days' – or were they?* 73
I   *An island life that is no longer* 79
J   *That's pretty steep!* 87
K   *Twinning makes the strain* 97
L   *'I'm from Brum!'* 107
M   *Sardines!* 113
N   *Phew!* 121
O   *Corks!* 129
P   *A tour de force?* 137
Q   *Belle Île or bust!* 147
R   *Althing's for all men?* 155
S   *Schier delight!* 165
T   *...the farther you go, the farther you still have to go!* 175
U   *Bator late than never?* 183
V   *Plan B to the end of the world* 193
W   *As one life reaches its climax, two others begin* 201
Y   *Faith in the future* 209
Z   *If the opposite of 'uncouth' is 'couth', so the opposite*
    of 'out of kilter' must be 'in'. 217
Epilogue 227
Acknowledgments 228

PREFACE
to the Second Edition

The *Little Green Nightbook* was my first book, an original concept which I was encouraged to proceed with by the well-known travel writer and expert Simon Calder. In the thirteen years since its appearance, this sequel – *Blue* – has followed, and a third collection – *Orange*.

Among the additions in this second edition of *Blue* is the inclusion of national, and where possible regional, flags at the start of each story to offer a further clue as to where the story is located. There are many new colour photos and illustrations to enhance the book's visual interest, ruled out in 2013 due to expense.

A full explanation of how these accounts of my travels came to be written appears in the Preface to the 2nd edition of the *Little Green Nightbook* (q.v.), rendering it superfluous to repeat here. However, it is perhaps useful to remind readers that the *Nightbooks* are written as entertainment and have no serious message. The only connection between one story and the next is that at some point in the past seventy years the events recounted happened to me. One can, therefore, look at the Contents page and choose to read the stories in any order.

Other travel books are detailed inside the front cover. The history series on local politics are eye-witness accounts and have been purchased by Southampton, my first university, for their library.

At the Winchester International Writers' Conference in 2013 the first of the political histories was awarded a 'Highly Commended' and an extract from the first draft of *Jottings from the Trans-Siberian Railway* was described by the adjudicator as 'a brilliantly written account of a very long journey' and received third prize.

M.K.

Author's Note: If a word is followed by an asterisk (*) it means it will appear in the Guide to Pronunciation at the end of the chapter.

INTRODUCTION

The *Little Green Nightbook*, first published in May 2010, was intended to introduce readers to the first of what might well become a trilogy of collections of personal anecdotes, of which this volume is the second to appear. Whatever may be said of the variety, interest or whimsy of the stories in the first volume, those in this one will be equal *(you have been warned!)*. Great care was taken not to put all the 'best' stories in the more outlandish locations in the first – '*Green*' – 'nightbook', thereby condemning the subsequent colours to carry all the dross. If you enjoyed the *Little Green Nightbook*, you will equally enjoy this one, its first successor.

The idea of writing up these reminiscences in the hope that they might be entertaining to other people occurred to me in 2003 when, having lost my seat on the local borough council for a second time and having by then notched up twenty years' service, I decided that it was an appropriate moment to call it a day. The village I represented was five miles from my home, and if I went to visit someone at the far end it was a round trip of twenty miles (and sometimes when I got there they'd be out, so it would be a wasted journey to boot). I reckoned I'd done my stint, and henceforth I'd do my politics where I lived – meaning that if I was out delivering leaflets and it started to rain I could nip back home and have a coffee and read the paper or make a phone call while interfering with the cat, instead of having to sit in the car in a lay-by twiddling my thumbs waiting for the weather to clear.

The first story I wrote was about how, driving in rural Brittany with my wife, Margaret, (now, sadly, my *late* wife, as she died in the summer of 2011) we were merely passing through an unremarkable village we'd never heard of when we noticed that it had two churches. One, though built in Gothic style, looked fairly modern and we knew from experience that in such buildings there's rarely anything of interest to a tourist; but the other church, apparently derelict, had a bent spire. This aroused our curiosity. We parked the car and went to look more closely, and the story about what befell us there appeared in the *Little Green Nightbook* under the little village's name *(and no, I'm not going to give the game away by saying what it was! You'll have to read the book and come across it)*. When I finished writing that story, methought 'I have a lot more stories like that in my memory bank. Some are comparatively recent, often driving around France with Margaret, but some date from my student days in the 1950s when the world was a very different place and my adventures (if one can glamorise them enough to call them that) took place at a time when Europe was still recovering from the ravages of the Second World War. My experiences, escapades, balls-ups even, took place in conditions which no longer pertain and can't be replicated. A modern reader might find them entertaining simply because they are being told against a backdrop which is totally alien to what a contemporary traveller in those places would experience now.' The other thought was, 'When I die, these stories will die with me. So better get them down on paper!'

In the Introduction to the *Little Green Nightbook* I explained in jocular detail who I was, my family and social background, experience of life and so on, to give the reader some sort of mind's-eye picture of where – as the cliché goes – I was 'coming from' and to emphasise to him or her that the book had no serious purpose or 'message' and was intended solely to entertain. This volume is a companion to its predecessor, so rather than repeat my biography I would respectfully advise anyone anxious to know something about *me* to 'read all about it!' as set out in the previous book. This may sound suspiciously like a ruse to sell more copies – but I assure you I speak in good faith. Someone who's read the *Little Green Nightbook* and is now moving on to the *Blue* one won't want to read again all that guff about my family, education, national service etc. etc. et bloody cetera.

The *Little Green Nightbook* carried a firm request – let's face it: strict instructions! – not to read it straight through but one story at a time prior to turning off the bedside light and going to sleep. Same again here: to get the most pleasure from the *Little Blue Nightbook* you should as before exercise iron self-control and not read it straight through like a novel, but take it one letter at a time each night. No story bears any connection either in time or place with the previous or following one – they are all free-standing, and designed to take the reader – with his or her connivance – to who-knows-where, who-knows-when. As there is no continuity, nothing is gained from reading one story and then proceeding straight to the next in the hope of maintaining the story line – there simply isn't one! The only common factor linking two consecutive stories is that they happened to me in the place and at the time indicated, either alone or with a companion.

Enjoy!

Goodnight.

The first story begins, unsurprisingly, with the letter A.
But that's for tomorrow.
Like I said – *goodnight!*

A

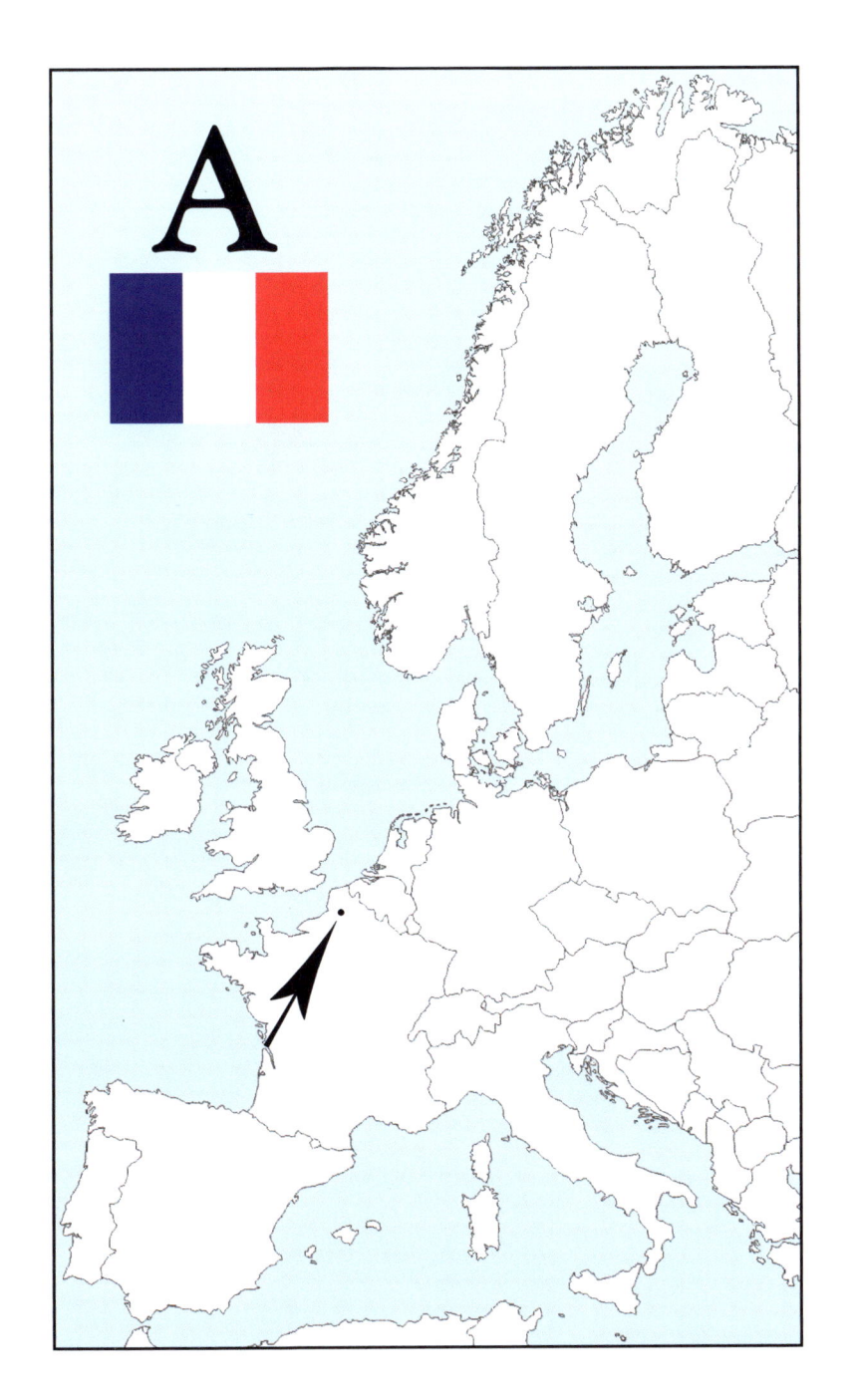

AGINCOURT

In at the beginning

[Conversations in italics were in French]

'*Who are the couple at the end of the table?*' I asked my host, the Mayor of Harfleur. The Fête de la Scie was over for another year. We were finishing a busy day in typical French fashion, around the table in a local restaurant. The other guests, apart from ourselves, were all Harfleur councillors or their spouses whom I knew from previous visits. Except for one couple.

'*She's a member of the council from Azincourt*', said Michel, interrupting.

Our host, Gérard, the mayor, nodded.

'*Why are they here?*' I asked.

'*We're working on an idea for mutual co-operation in promoting our tourism, something along the lines of English visitors interested in the Hundred Years' War coming here to see where Henry V started his campaign in 1415 when he laid siege to our town and then set off for Calais to take his army home and ended up facing our King on the battlefield at what you English call Agincourt. You know the rest.*'

'*Will you introduce us?*'

The result was that I got into conversation with the village councillor from Azincourt who, accompanied by her husband, was also a civic guest at Harfleur's fête. Azincourt is only a tiny village, with a population of some 300 people. They get as many as 15,000 English tourists in a year, far more than they can cope with, all wanting to see the site where on 25 October 1415 one of the decisive battles of the Hundred Years' War took place, a battle which everyone in England has heard of if not through school history lessons then through Shakespeare's play – which they probably know through the famous film starring Laurence Olivier or its more recent re-make by Kenneth Branagh.

'*Harfleur's Act I of Henry's journey*', she told me. '*We're the finale. Perhaps our two councils together could work up a tourist trail designed for English visitors to start here in Harfleur, follow Henry's route and end up with us, stopping en route at other villages or small towns where he threatened the local people, took the surrender of their castle, attempted to cross the Somme and so on.'*

It sounded like an idea worth examining. Henry V is one of England's most famous medieval kings, and tourists would be interested in visiting places where important events during his reign took place; in particular, they would all know about the siege of Harfleur and the Battle of Agincourt and, given a bit of help and encouragement, would like to visit both of them. An increase in tourist numbers would boost the local economy, so both places would benefit if they got together and offered some sort of package along the lines of 'With Henry V to Agincourt!'.

The councillor from Azincourt was equally puzzled by our presence.

'What brings you two to Harfleur? I thought English tourists all went to Honfleur. Did you make a mistake and mix them up?'

'No. We've been to Honfleur on several occasions, but today we're here in Harfleur as the mayor's guests. We come from Eastleigh, which is as close to Southampton as Harfleur is to Le Havre and he thought we might face similar problems marketing ourselves as he does, both of us being, so to speak, overshadowed by a larger neighbour and he might learn something by talking to us. Basically, what he wanted to do was pick our brains. So he wrote to our tourist office and they invited him to come over with some of his colleagues – councillors and officials. We entertained them during their visit as we're both councillors and Margaret's portfolio includes responsibility for promoting Eastleigh's tourism. They invited us back during their annual Fête de la Scie, and we've been coming most years ever since – at our own expense, mind – and that's why we're here now.'

But this is supposed to be about Agincourt. Enough of Harfleur But you would enjoy their spring Fête, so go if you can. It's usually the first week-end in April.

You may have noticed two different spellings; Agincourt is the English version of the name of a village which on French maps is spelled not with a *g* but a *z*. The story goes that in the aftermath of the battle Henry asked someone where they were, and when told the name of the château visible on the horizon told his secretary to use it. Unfortunately the man wrote it down with a "g" instead, and it's stayed that way in English ever since. But if you're planning to go there, don't go looking for "Agincourt" with a g on a French map!

The lady councillor from Azincourt then explained why she and her husband were here in Harfleur.

'When visitors arrive they are disappointed because there's really nothing to see – just a field – so we decided that what we needed is a proper museum. But not your ordinary local museum with a few rusty halberds laid out in display cases and pictures of knights in armour. Azincourt's a bit special, and the site of one of the major battles between us and the English during The Hundred Years' War. We need a proper visitor centre explaining to visitors what medieval life was like, how people lived, how they fought, what their weapons were like and what skills and techniques were required to use them effectively.

Equally important, a proper visitor centre could explain to people of today why kings in medieval times apparently spent so much of their time fighting and then invited their erstwhile enemies to banquets and displays and married off female members of their immediate family to each other. Exhibits could show the political map of Europe at the beginning of the fifteenth century and how different it is from today's. What court life was like. Explain, showing historical documents, what relations were like between nobles and kings and nobles and each other, including when fighting each other and when not.

No way could we in tiny Azincourt afford to build such a centre, so the money has had to come from the département and the French government. In fact, several million euros have been spent on creating a showcase 'medieval experience', and we're having the official opening in three months time. Would you like to come?'

You bet!

So three months later, at the end of June and bearing presents as well as our official invitation from the mayor of Azincourt, we booked ourselves into Les 3 Luppars in Arras and drove to the village for the grand opening ceremony. The new centre, I'm bound to say, is truly amazing, and very well thought through. The entrance is designed to look like a row of bows pointing skywards with arrows notched, the view that the French knights at the start of the battle would have had of the front row of Henry's archers, bows 'loaded' just waiting for the order to loose. This architectural bull's-eye underlines the importance at that time of the longbow, the contemporary weapon of mass destruction. In the battle it was the English archers' mastery of this new powerful weapon coupled with Henry's mastery of tactics which enabled them to cut down the flower of the French nobility and gave the English a most unexpected victory in a contest where they were outnumbered three or four to one and the French were over-confident.

Michel had been invited to represent Harfleur at the opening ceremony and we succeeded in finding him in the crowd before the formal ceremony started. This consisted of lengthy speeches, but I managed to sneak out of the marquee and go round the exhibits. One of Margaret's persistent complaints about visiting museums

Azincourt Visitor Centre

with me was that I want to read every word of every label, which is all the more irritating for her when they're in French and I have difficulty in translating specialist historical terms. No one seems to have thought of publishing a specialised dictionary for foreigners who visit French museums, as the usual pocket variety doesn't have room for words for the individual bits of a knight's armour. When I was at school we had a joke about what comprised essential French phrases, and we all tried to think up the most unlikely, e.g. 'Lo! The postillion has been struck by lightning' and 'I've left my theodolite in the belfry'. But a glossary of technical and historical terms on a bi-lingual hand-out from museum reception would help.

I'm bound to say that in this exhibition the curatorial staff have got it absolutely right: both languages are used, but the French versions are much longer than the English. This is because the French are trying to explain to their own, French, tourists all about the contemporary situation in France at the time and the politics of the wars, whereas English visitors, with perhaps less time available, only really want to know what something is, who somebody is or what's happening in the picture. They reckon, I suppose, that English tourists with a serious interest in the history of that period can probably read French anyway, so there's no need to put all the details in English.

I judged from the distant sound of applause when the ceremonial speeches were over and it was safe to return to the crowd in the marquee and avail myself of a drink. We sought out the mayor and presented him with a print of the Westgate in Southampton, through which Henry V passed when he embarked on the campaign. Thus he had a picture of where Henry started, to hang in his office at the place where it ended. On our return to England later that week we submitted a story and picture to our local paper the *Hampshire Chronicle*, and sent him a copy. He did not acknowledge receipt and we never heard another word, but that's the French for you.

The battlefield itself is just farmland, but there are some interesting attempts by means of life-size two-dimensional men-at-arms positioned at the crossroads or peering at you from roadside hedgerows to tell the tale of what happened on this spot six hundred years ago. One can hardly expect the French to 'celebrate' a battle which they so comprehensively lost when they had overwhelming numerical superiority and should have won, but facts are facts. Azincourt is the site of a famous battle which had profound repercussions at the time and the only thing which prevented Henry succeeding in his ambition of uniting France and England under one king – himself – was that he contracted dysentery and died at the early age of 35, contrary to all expectations pre-deceasing Charles VI of France by six weeks. But because he died when he did and the English campaign faltered, the 1420s belong not to England inspired by Henry but to France inspired by Joan of

Arc. France was rescued from the invader and the French for their part had something to celebrate: the raising of the siege of Orléans by the Maid and the crowning of their own king, Charles VII, in the cathedral at Reims in defiance of the English who had crowned Henry V's infant son Henry VI as King of France at Rouen.

The author presents the Mayor of Azincourt with a print of the Westgate in Southampton.

Odd that a chance meeting in a restaurant in Harfleur should result in us being present at an important cultural and historic event: the opening of the Azincourt visitor centre!

June 2001

A new twist to the phrase 'An arrow pointing to the parking area'!

POSTSCRIPT
It is well known that the French have a lot of trouble with their feet, so much so that they even have a special phrase to describe it: *'Chacun a son goût'* – 'Each has his gout'.

Goodnight.

B

BIEŻANÓW*

A Window on the East
(with acknowledgements to Peter the Great)

In my student days I belonged to an organisation called International Voluntary Service for Peace (IVSP. Later they dropped the "P"). Volunteers were often students during vacations, but some were older and there were even full-timers, who devoted their whole lives to the organisation and were paid a small salary. Before being allowed to join a camp overseas a prospective volunteer had to take part in at least one camp in his or her home country, just to make sure that they had the essential 'volunteer' frame of mind, were prepared to work conscientiously unsupervised and could fit in with an international group where the working language of the camp might not be their own. The bargain was simple: food and accommodation were provided free by the host organisation you were doing the work for, but you received no pay. How you made the journey from your home to the camp was your business – IVSP didn't pay anyone's fare. Most of us hitch-hiked. Having served my probationary stint in England (as recounted in the *Little Green Nightbook, q.v.*), I volunteered for a camp on the continent. As luck would have it, IVSP had just successfully concluded lengthy and difficult negotiations to set up a joint East-West camp with volunteers from both sides of the Iron Curtain working together. It was to be in Poland. I jumped at the chance as I had just graduated and was seeking funding for a PhD in Polish history.

The pioneer East-West camp was just outside Kraków at a small place called Bieżanów, so my route would take me by train to Strasbourg and then on the Paris-Warsaw express across Czechoslovakia. I recall quite clearly my first crossing of the Czech border because it was so utterly different compared to 46 years later on a coach going to Prague for the Christmas market. My first time was by train across the border at Cheb through a deep cutting and when I looked up I saw the muzzle of a sentry's sub-machine gun sticking out from the top of the watchtower and glinting in the sun. The border between East and West was heavily delineated, with two high barbed wire parallel fences stretching to the horizon in both directions and the land between them mined, we were assured, and armed patrols all the way along under orders to shoot anyone trying to cross. By contrast, the border between Czechoslovakia and Poland appeared to be nothing but a line of ploughed furrows in a field and there was minimal delay with frontier formalities. Who, after all, was likely to be stowing away to get out of Communist Czechoslovakia into Communist Poland? On the other hand, there was a popular joke at the time about a dog running across from Czechoslovakia into Poland who meets another dog coming the other way.

'Why are you leaving Poland?' asks the Czech dog.

'I'm going to Czechoslovakia to have a good feed', says the Polish dog, 'Why are you leaving Czechoslovakia?'

'I'm going to Poland to have a good bark.'

To get the joke, bitter as it is, if you consider the implied differences in how the Communist dictatorships in the two countries functioned you can work it out for yourself, even though it's no longer appropriate. The Iron Curtain is long gone, and now both Czechs and Poles live in democracies.

Leaving the train at Kraków* I immediately faced a problem experienced in those days by every independent traveller: because it was not permitted to have Polish currency, zlotys, outside Poland I had absolutely no Polish money. OK perhaps if you were a businessman and took a taxi from the airport to your hotel and the driver waited outside while you changed a traveller's cheque at reception. I was travelling alone by public transport with nothing but a rucksack, and what I needed when I left the station was the equivalent of about fourpence for the bus fare to the hostel I was booked into. I explained this as best I could to the ticket collector, who I realised afterwards must have heard it many times before from odd bods arriving from the West penniless because of his own country's strict currency regulations. But he smiled, explained where the hostel was and which bus to catch and then put his hand in his pocket and gave me the fare. I don't suppose he ever realised just what a fillip his spontaneous action gave to Anglo-Polish relations, and that I would be recalling his kindness to a total stranger over fifty years after the event.

In case you're wondering how I managed to communicate at all, let me explain. I was aware that despite communist propaganda about all the peoples in Eastern Europe loving the Russians for freeing them from Nazi tyranny in fact most Poles loathed them, but as I was immediately recognisable from my appearance as being from the West (to start with, I had a beard), and as no Pole would expect a Westerner to speak Polish it was actually quite acceptable for me to speak Russian as the next best thing. But this created an interesting dilemma: no one ever *answered* me in Russian! Older people in southern Poland who had been to school in the days when it was part of the Austro-Hungarian Empire would reply in German, hoping I would know that language as well; others in default of knowing any English would use bits of whatever Western language they'd picked up. I remember a positively surreal conversation in a bookshop in Warsaw a few weeks later, when I asked in Russian for a particular book displayed in the window, the shop assistant replied slowly in Polish and refused to be deflected. She obviously understood every word I said (after all, Russian was compulsory in Polish schools at that time), but absolutely no way would she speak Russian to me even though it would have made everything so much easier. It was extremely illuminating about how ordinary Poles really felt towards their saviours. But I got the book.

Visitors from the West were not common in Poland in the mid-fifties, so at the hostel I was soon the centre of attention for local students eager to have their first-ever conversation in English with a native speaker. They were very keen to grill me about life in the West, and were fully aware that it wasn't anything like the picture painted by official propaganda. Ida*, a student at the Jagiełłonian University but originally from Szczecin*, gave me her address, and we exchanged letters for a couple of years. Jacek* and Leszek* volunteered to take me to my final destination next day, Bieżanów being about twenty minutes by bus from Kraków. Getting this far had not been uneventful, and there was more to come.

The camp had not been organised by IVSP's HQ in London but by our Belgian branch, which meant that the working language of the camp was French. This widened my language experience, in particular when they got the cards out one evening after work and, discovering I could play bridge, proceeded to teach me how to bid in French. Our work consisted of levelling ground for a railway manoeuvring depot, which was not the sort of work IVSP would normally agree to do. The camp leader explained that they were keen to make contacts across the Iron Curtain and it was this or nothing. In the West IVSP volunteers did manual work of a socially useful nature, helping disadvantaged groups. In the communist paradise in the East, of course, there *were* no disadvantaged groups.

In the face of obstinate official refusal to admit that there was any requirement for the sort of work organisations such as ours normally did, what they had offered us was all we were going to get. The leaders of IVSP swallowed hard, I suppose, and accepted the deal as the only way of getting a foothold in Eastern Europe. It was a departure from normal practice, but then running the first-ever camp in a communist country with young people from both sides of the Iron Curtain living and working together was not normal practice, either. The pay-off was getting a foot in the door, so to speak, and the hope that we could help improve mutual understanding and in due course organise a parallel East-West camp in the West, with East Europeans being allowed to travel to take part.

In the Tatra Mountains with Jim Riordan from England (l) and Palle Rossen (r) from Denmark

With my new Polish friends (I am second on the left).

*The Black Wall, Auschwitz, where inmates were lined up and shot.
An urn of flowers is placed in front as a memorial*

Our working day began at seven, and there was a rota each morning to rise at five for a half-hour tramp across the fields to a farm to collect milk for breakfast. We went in pairs, one who'd made the trip the day before to show the newcomer the way, and then the newcomer did the old hand bit the next day and so on until we'd all taken our turn. We worked, pick and shovel, until two, and went back to our hut for dinner. When there was a sudden downpour which flooded our work area we were put instead to moving an enormous pile of bricks hand-to-hand in a human chain. The rest of the day was our own, and the Polish members of our camp organised group visits to Kraków to see the sights in one of the most beautiful medieval cities you could wish for and to meet other young people for more East-West contact. They also arranged visits to the salt mines at Wieliczka*, to Zakopane* in the Tatra Mountains near the Czech border and to another place of interest in the vicinity which under its Polish name of Oświęcim doesn't strike a chord but is infamous when said in the German version: Auschwitz.

With my shovel (foreground) I had a mountain to move!

The duration of the camp was two weeks, and having made no plans for my return home I set off for Warsaw where I had heard that it was possible to hitch a lift to Gdynia on the British Embassy lorry which made the journey every week to collect supplies for the staff, many foodstuffs and what to us were ordinary household items being unobtainable in Poland at that time. I was joined on this leg of my journey by Kirsten, a Danish girl I had palled up with at the camp, who assured me that there were Danish cargo boats at Gdynia scraping a living from what little trade there was between Denmark and Poland. We struck a bargain: I would do the talking at the embassy and get us both a lift on the official lorry, and when we got to Gdynia she would find us a Danish ship and fix a passage to Copenhagen.

Sitting in the cab of the lorry I had a grandstand view of the Polish countryside, and was struck by the large number of horse-drawn farm wagons on the road whenever we approached a town. They were farmers taking produce to market, too poor to have cars, lorries or even tractors. We arrived in Gdynia, but in the meantime Kirsten had decided that she wasn't yet ready to leave Poland and her new-found Polish boyfriend and so would not be crossing the Baltic with me after all. But she kept her side of the bargain and found me a ship.

'You come with us to Denmark?' asked the captain. 'That'll be £5.'

For his return voyage the only cargo the skipper had been able to find was birch strips for binding barrels of butter. They weighed almost nothing, so with inadequate ballast we were high in the water. In consequence, we rolled and pitched in the Baltic swell and I retired to my bunk to avoid letting the side down by publicly succumbing to seasickness, and stayed there until we docked the next day.

'You haven't eaten anything!' said the skipper, as I prepared to disembark – and gave me £3 back.

It was Sunday morning, a wonderfully bright, sunny August day. I was the only traveller going through customs, and the duty officer who stamped my passport seemed rather surprised at this rather scruffy Englishman with his rucksack coming into his country from sort of the wrong direction, i.e. from Poland. But no questions were asked, he just stamped me as entering the country and I set off to find a bed for the night before exploring the city the next day.

July 1958

Guide to Pronunciation

Biezanów	B-yeh-*zhar*-noof
Ida	*Ee*-da
Jacek	*Yats*-ek
Kraków	*Krak*-oof
Leszek	*Lesh*-ek
Oświęcim	Osh-*vyen*-tseem
Szczecin	*Shchet*-seen
Wieliczka	V-yell-*eech*-ka
Zakopane	*Zak*-op-arn-eh

POSTSCRIPT
He who laughs last – has not seen the joke.

Goodnight.

C

CANTERBURY

'...to Caunterbury they wende' (Chaucer)

Margaret didn't feel up to taking me abroad as my birthday treat – her doctor had forbidden her to fly and in February we had foregone our customary week at our time-share in Lanzarote. My natal day is in mid-March, and whereas one year she'd taken up a special offer in our local paper to take me to Dinan for the weekend this time she suggested a jaunt to Canterbury as a less stressful alternative – especially as it would be me doing the driving and there wouldn't be the physical demands associated with the ferry crossing. She'd always wanted to see the cathedral but had never managed it. My only visit was a whistle-stop half a century ago.

What probably decided her was an advert in our daily paper by a new hotel actually situated in the cathedral precincts, offering weekend stays at knock-down prices and including free parking and free admission to the cathedral itself. A booking there would enable us to solve an anticipated problem with parking, which even out of season is not likely to be easily resolvable in a city which attracts foreign tourists in their thousands to see the site where Roman Christianity first established itself in England in 597 when Pope Gregory the Great sent St Augustine on a mission to convert the pagan Saxons. He chose his opportunity well, for although King Ethelbert of Kent was a heathen his wife Queen Bertha was a Christian and had her own chaplain and the use of a church in which to pray daily.

Canterbury may boast England's oldest and most important cathedral, but finding it presented unexpected problems. Unlike many other cathedrals it doesn't have a spire – compare, in particular, Salisbury, whose spire rises 123m / 404ft and in its day was the tallest building in England. Canterbury's cathedral is almost completely quarantined from the town by an unbroken defensive wall of tall buildings which in former times protected it against attack while providing living and working space for the clerks when the Church provided the royal civil service and the archbishop was a principal advisor to the King and from time to time his Chancellor. The Church's power is much diminished in our day, but even if the buildings which surround the cathedral to keep out the mob are no longer required for administrative functions – lay or ecclesiastical – they are still there, effectively hiding it from public view. Our hotel advertised that it was located in the cathedral grounds – but we couldn't find the cathedral!

Entering from the west by the medieval gateway and following signs and the old walls, we eventually got into the city itself and spotted an access road into the cathedral precincts, but a sign clearly told us 'Authorised traffic only'. We interpreted this to mean people on church business, so we continued on our way and found ourselves right in the middle of the town's fully pedestrianised centre driving on a road reserved solely for delivery or emergency vehicles – and just as the local secondary school was disgorging its pupils! 'What now?' 'MIND THAT CHILD!' 'How the hell do we get out?' 'What happens when a traffic warden spots us and we get booked?' Surprising how you sweat in a crisis – especially when you're in a crowded place where you know you shouldn't be and are the unwanted focus of attention.

As luck would have it, there were a couple of traffic wardens patrolling, so I drove over to them and wound down the window. 'We're strangers, and we're lost! How do we get out? We're booked into a hotel in the cathedral precincts, but we can't find a road in, so how do we get to it?' She explained. 'But it's marked 'Authorised traffic only'. 'You're staying at the hotel?' 'Yes.' 'Then you're authorised.' 'Oh.' Makes sense when you think about it, but it would be a great improvement if they added another sign saying 'Hotel **** access for guests' or some such to avoid misunderstandings. Driving in the pedestrianised zone was embarrassing, to say the least – and I'm sure we weren't the first visitors who made the same mistake.

Christ Church Gateway, Canterbury Cathedral
(photo courtesy of the Chapter of Canterbury Cathedral)

We were surprised at how comparatively small the centre of Canterbury is, and the limited number of top class places for a proper lunch or dinner. A couple were housed in old buildings and there were some pleasant continental restaurants where we ate well enough, but for such a major tourist hub we just expected to be tripping over them. Maybe the damage done by World War II bombs was more decisive, and cafés and restaurants can make more money catering for the lower end of the market – students and back-packers. But then medieval pilgrims didn't always have very much money, so the present-day pattern in supplying comestibles is probably the outcome of centuries of experience.

The first historic building we visited after doing a full tour of the cathedral was the Eastridge museum, which soon after the murder of St Thomas à Becket in the cathedral in 1170 was built as a place to stay for poor pilgrims visiting his shrine.

Eastridge Museum

The underground Roman museum fascinated us, the result of one of the aforesaid bombs leaving a crater and revealing to public view for the first time in almost two millennia the existence of a Roman house. Its mosaic floors are still in their original positions, and overall the exhibits are very well laid out, with clear explanations – a model for us all – and lots of question papers and games for children. The Chaucer Experience – if I can call it that – was totally different. To be visited with tongue well stuffed into cheek, but enjoyable in its light-hearted take on medieval life – bedbugs and all – and the tribulations of the then prevailing *modus vivendi*. But unless you are familiar with the text of *The Canterbury Tales* you won't get all the jokes.

Wandering idly, we attracted the unexpected attentions of a punter touting for business – a real one, selling tickets for a trip on his punt. We'd not expected such an essentially summertime activity to be on offer so early in the season. Maybe it was a fine day and he thought he might get lucky and attract some bonus punters? (*Sorry!*). Replete with straw boater and virtually non-stop explanation of flora and fauna, he did an excellent job, all the time either standing to punt us along the canal or sitting to row us when he reached the river – and warning us well in time to lie back flat on our cushions when approaching a low bridge. What was particularly disarming was that as a combination of boatman and natural history guide he knew his stuff and appeared to be enthusiastically enjoying himself as well as serving his customers.

Leaving Canterbury to make our way home we'd arranged to stop off near Ashford to visit two old friends from our university days, Arthur and Marian. The singular fact about Marian is that she is the only person I am still in contact with who was actually at school with me – we go back that far. When I went up to university after completing my national service who should be at the top of the steps up to the West Building – the student part of the university – on my first day but Marian – who at school I'd known by her first name, which she would prefer not to be made public so we'll stick to her second name. 'It's Martin Kyrle! What are you doing here?' 'It's ***** Palmer! What are you doing here?' 'Same as you, and I'm not called ***** any more, I'm called Marian'. 'Right'.

We were thrown together mainly through our membership of

the university's Operatic Society. In the spring of my first year we put on HMS *Pinafore*, with me in the chorus and Marian in the role of Little Buttercup. Later Arthur came on the scene and we staged *Cox and Box* with me as Cox and Arthur playing Sergeant Bouncer, the landlord. Marian is bigger-built than Arthur and a couple of inches taller, and when I learned of them pairing up I asked her confidentially, 'Who carries the stool?', as for her the description 'little' in 'Little Buttercup' was – and is – entirely inappropriate. But they were soon clearly getting serious, and one day during a rehearsal Marian took me to one side and whispered in my ear, 'I wish they made Arthurs in larger sizes'. It didn't stop them going the whole hog and getting married and having two daughters, and at the present time they've been married for fifty-four years.

Another memory of our student G & S productions was what happened in *Patience*. I was the producer and Marian had the part of Lady Jane, one of Gilbert's standard contralto roles of an older woman losing her looks and desperate for a husband, and set up to be the butt of some heavy-handed sarcasm on stage. There's a well-known comic duet with one of the male leads, Bunthorne, which when it ends and the two singers have left the stage it's by custom encored and they perform it again but instead of just walking off at the end make their exit in some absurd way just for laughs. In our production, for the first encore Marian went into the wings and came back with a wheelbarrow, shoved Bunthorne into it and pushed him off with his legs kicking wildly (uproar!). Follow that! She did. They came on for the second encore and at the end she grabbed Bunthorne, threw him over her shoulder and marched off stage carrying him in a fireman's lift, arms and legs waving frantically. Brought the house down.

Marian comes from Fareham and is a life-long Labour supporter, following her father who was an unsuccessful council candidate until right at the end of his life when he finally got elected but died soon after. Our conversations, therefore, have always veered into politics, and in former times converged around the pointlessness of her being Labour in a place like Fareham and me being a Liberal practically anywhere. Things changed when I won a seat on the

Members of

Southampton University Operatic Society

present

COX AND BOX
(Triumviretta in One Act)

by

F. C. Burnand and Sir Arthur Sullivan

(By Permission of Bridget D'Oyly Carte)

and

The TELEPHONE
(Opera Buffa)

by

Gian-Carlo Menotti

at

8.0 p.m.

in the

UNIVERSITY THEATRE

26th - 27th - 28th - JUNE, 1958

The Entertainment will commence with the arrival of the Queen of Sheba.

'COX and BOX'

Directed by:
IAN THOMAS

Dramatis personae:

JAMES JOHN COX	A Journeyman Hatter	MARTIN KYRLE
JOHN JAMES BOX	A Journeyman Printer	BRIAN KEITH-SMITH
SERGEANT BOUNCER	A Lodging House Keeper—with military reminiscences	ARTHUR BARKER

SCENE: A room in Sergeant Bouncer's Establishment.

TIME: Late nineteenth century.

The action takes place in the lodging house kept by Sergeant Bouncer, and concerns his efforts to conceal from his two lodgers the fact that, unbeknown to them, they share the same room! His ruse is discovered when Mr. Cox unexpectedly receives a day's holiday, and returns home to find a stranger (Mr. Box) in his room. After initial misunderstandings, including a concertina solo, a challenge to a duel and a "dulcet dirge," the two lodgers discover that among their many things in common is their parentage, and decide to continue sharing the room.

There will then be an INTERVAL of five minutes, followed by a CONCERT (devised and directed by Martin Kyrle), which will begin with

L'Arlésienne—Farandole   (*Bizet*)   The Accompanists

Based on a play by Daudet and first produced in 1872, "L'Arlésienne" tells of the love of a Provençal farmer for an unworthy dancer from Arles. The farandole consists of the alternation and ultimate combination of two themes—a march and a Provençal dance.

Marriage of Figaro---Voi Che Sapete   (*Mozart*)   Hilary Taylor

Cherubino sings this in Act II complaining to Susanna that ladies take no notice of him as he is so young.

On 26-28 June 1958 —

Cavalleria Rusticana—Romance and Scene (*Mascagni*) Rosemary Storkey
The scene is the square of a Sicilian village, where Santuzza sings of how she has been betrayed by Turiddu. Before he went away to the wars Turiddu had been in love with Lola who, having tired of waiting for him to return, has now married Alfio, the village carrier. Discovering this on his return, Turiddu turns to Santuzza, but discards her to return to Lola, taking advantage of Alfio's frequent absences on business.

The Barber of Seville—Largo al factotum (*Rossini*) Ian Thomas
Dating from 1816, this well-known comic opera revolves around the machinations of that loveable rogue, Figaro. In this famous aria he laments the hardships of the life of a barber and general jack-of-all-trades, who never has a moment's peace!

Tales of Hoffman—Doll Song (*Offenbach*) Hilary Taylor
Olympia, described as Spalanzani the doll-maker's daughter, is presented to her "father's" guests, and in singing to them reveals the automaton-like delivery one might expect from a mechanical toy which has to be continually wound up.

Carmen—Toreador's Song (*Bizet*) Brian Keith-Smith
It is the beginning of Act II; the scene—a tavern. There are shouts from without: "Long live Escamillo!" Enter the toreador—a debonair figure in his fine costume, and the idol of the crowd.

Samson and Delila—Delila's Song (*Saint-Saens*) Marian Palmer
In this song, Delila calls to the Philistines to enter Samson's house and trap him.

Die Zauberflöte—Duet, Act II (*Mozart*) Marian Palmer
Ivor Levinson
After almost despairing of ever finding his lover, Papageno, the bird-catcher, is told by the Genii to set his magic bells ringing. When he does so his love Papagena appears, and the two sing of their happiness at being reunited.

Rigoletto—La Donna è mobile (*Verdi*) Martin Kyrle
Gilda who has been jilted by the Duke, sees him go into a tavern and sing this buoyant song over his wine—so much in keeping with the Duke's character.

Merrie England—The Waltz Song (*German*) Hilary Taylor
This is Bessie's song from Act II in praise of the delights of love.

The Desert Song (*Romberg*) Brian Keith-Smith
This is the theme song from the well-known operetta.

Die Zauberflöte—In diesen Leiligen Hallen (*Mozart*) Ivor Levinson
The High-Priest Zoroaster here tells of the glory and riches of the halls of wisdom over which he rules, protected by the shield of light.

INTERVAL of 10 minutes

---

all three of us were on stage —

'THE TELEPHONE'

Produced by:
BRIAN KEITH-SMITH

Dramatis personae:

LUCY ROSEMARY STORKEY
BEN IAN THOMAS

SCENE: Lucy's apartment in New York.
TIME: The present.

First produced in 1947 in New York, " The Telephone " is usually seen as a curtain-raiser to Menotti's longer work " The Medium." The action takes place in Lucy's apartment while Ben is trying to propose to her. He is continually thwarted by calls on the telephone, and in despair has to rush off to catch a train. Taking a last chance, he telephones Lucy from the station and proposes. This time the telephone is his friend.

Stage Manager	JOHN TAYLOR
Paintings by	KIRSTEN THOMPSON
Wardrobe Mistress	CELIA PHILLIPS
Make-Up by	BRIAN LEWIS
Lighting by	MIKE RUSSELL, JOHN LANE, PAT WOOSTER, PETER LANIGAN
Prompter	VARIOUS
Front-of-House Manager	IAN PURVIS
Front-of-House Manager	MARGARET ROUND
Treasurer	IVOR FASTCAR
Publicity Manager	IAN THOMAS
Programme compiled by	MARTIN KYRLE
Accompanists	KENNETH BROOKS, PETER LAMBERT
Musical Director:	RAYMOND TURLEY
Modern Furniture lent by	TYRRELL & GREEN LTD.
No Smoking by	REQUEST

Printed by G. F. WILSON & CO. LTD.

while Margaret (under her maiden name) was Front of House Manager council to join Margaret, who then progressed to become Mayor for the first time – even though my parliamentary ambitions came to nothing (four elections, four second places). The sad thing now is that both Marian and Arthur are suffering the ravages of old age, her with crippling osteoarthritis leaving her walking with two sticks and Arthur fighting vascular dementia. What makes the situation particularly poignant so far as I'm concerned is that they're both younger than me – though this is partly counterbalanced by the fact that at least they're both still alive, and older than Margaret was when she died. It's a funny old world, *innit*, and there just ain't no justice. But good to see them again, and reminisce over old times and audience reactions to our long-past and long-forgotten performances when we trod the boards.

> In the first edition of the *Little Blue Nightbook* a photo of Ightham Mote courtyard (taken by the author's wife) appeared. Two jobsworths employed by the National Trust insisted on a fee of £50 to use it again, so it doesn't appear. Dear reader, anyone with access to the internet can type 'Ightham Mote' and see it for free. Which is why the NT's demand for fifty quid was declined and this space is blank.
> In contrast, the Chapter of Canterbury Cathedral bent over backwards to source a new photo of Christ Church Gate when I rejected the first one they sent, and with never any suggestion of payment. They recognised the value of good publicity, unlike the NT whose employees' dogmatic attitude make it appear money-grubbing and insensitive.

To round off a lovely birthday weekend we made another diversion before heading for home: take the opportunity to visit Ightham Mote, a remarkable survival of a 14th century moated manor house which belongs to the National Trust and is so evocative and 'chocolate box perfect' that it frequently does precisely what you'd expect: it appears in pictures on boxes of chocolates. Off the beaten track in a secluded and heavily-wooded valley, it lay

half-forgotten for centuries and thus escaped modernisation and remains as it has always been, intact and entirely authentic.
   Goodnight.

March 2010

Authors' note: since the original publication, both Arthur and Marian have died.

POSTSCRIPT
Two kangaroos were hopping along together and one kept scratching her pouch.
Suddenly she stopped, and then reached inside and pulled out the joey and smacked his bottom.
Second kangaroo: 'Why did you do that?'
First kangaroo: 'I've told him before not to eat biscuits in bed.'

Goodnight.

D

43

DUBROVNIK

... and Plan A

It had taken us thirteen hours overnight on the train from Sarajevo when by dawn's early light we crested the hills outside Dubrovnik and saw a hillside covered with cypresses all standing like a medieval army with spears at the ready waiting for the order to attack, and beyond them the Adriatic. You can read about that under S *(though not in <u>this</u> book)*.

Dubrovnik was all it's cracked up to be, and you can get a brochure from your friendly neighbourhood travel agent if you want a guided tour. All I need say is that we enjoyed walking the walls and reading up a brand new subject: the history of the Republic of Ragusa. We then set about finding out how to make our way up the coast to Rijeka and on into Austria to reach the refugee camp at Linz where we were scheduled to start work in time to meet our deadline.

Before taking the ferry, we determined to have a swim. A mistake, as Bob almost immediately trod on a sea urchin, which was not amused and retaliated by leaving a load of its spines embedded in his foot. For the entire duration of the ferry ride up the coast, at any moment we were sitting down anywhere Bob would take off his sandal and commence picking at his foot with his penknife, trying to tease out yet another urchin spine. Not a pretty sight, but at least it kept other passengers away. Especially with me looking them straight in the eye while furtively pointing sideways at my clearly deranged companion, gazing upwards into the sky and shaking my head slowly. Bob claimed to have once got to the front of a queue in a chemist's shop by declaiming in a loud voice of his companion at the time, 'They must have *something* for the black palsy', whereupon everyone else in the shop turned pale and sidled out through the door, leaving Bob at the counter where he was able to ask for the bottle of aspirins he'd come for. But what else could you expect from someone who was the only boy in his class at school whose parents had no children?

Boarding the ferry was a free-for-all, but we'd worked out Plan A in advance – a version of which I still employ when travelling minus car but with wife. I would carry both our rucksacks, 'doing a donkey out of a job', as my grandfather used to say. Bob would go ahead unencumbered, get a ticket and weave his way through other passengers who were technically ahead of us in the queue and make for the point of the bow *(translation for landlubbers: up at the sharp end)*. He would there mark out our territory by taking off his coat, sandals or whatever to show that this bit was taken, with the implication that he was awaiting his friend who, let me warn you, is 18 stone, of unpredictable disposition when crossed and chews hammers as a hobby (*i.e. not a professional, but a hammer-chewer*). Baring his teeth and coughing convulsively or doing a bit more urchin spine-picking with an open penknife also helped keep other passengers at a safe distance. In due course I would arrive, nonchalantly sauntering at the back of the crowd of embarkees, and simply deposit the two rucksacks and sit down. Being as far for'ard as it was possible to get had the advantage that you had the gunwales to lean against and only had other passengers next to you on one side and no one trying to go past you as there was nowhere past you to go.

Our first stop was the island of Hvar, but not enough time to disembark and explore. Another time, perhaps. Then into harbour at Split, and an afternoon to kill. The Roman emperor Diocletian built a palace at Split, and why I remember it so well is that inside the walls there were various kiosks and one of them sold the finest ice cream I've ever tasted. It was also so hot that when we found the road was lined with palm trees we took to walking along each tree's shadow from root to canopy and then darting as quickly as possible in a straight line to the base of the next one and then repeating the zigzag manoeuvre. Must have looked a bit like a film take for 'The Invasion of the Crab-men', but when you're wearing clothing for all seasons, not stripped off in shirt-sleeves for a heat wave, you are pretty desperate to get out of the direct heat of the sun.

The Dalmatian Islands are very picturesque, and I made a mental note to come back one day and explore them at leisure. Again, I'm still waiting – nearly sixty years later.

Rijeka was an interesting place, and we had time to go shopping. In restaurants in Sarajevo and Dubrovnik I had drunk coffee made in the Turkish fashion in individual brass pots with long handles, and I was determined to buy a set to take home as a souvenir. Prices in tourist shops were beyond my pocket. We found ourselves in the local market, where the prices being charged by the craftsmen were even higher. Then a thought struck me: where do the locals buy theirs? Answer: in the ironmongery section of a general store. Indeed, the prices there were a small fraction of the others, and I duly acquired my souvenirs. For the remainder of my student years I was able to impress colleagues and numerous girlfriends with my genoo-ine bedou-ine Turkish coffee made in the authentic way and in the proper utensils – 'Oh', I'd reply laconically when asked where they came from. 'I picked these up during my travels in the Balkans'.

Travel snobs aren't new . . .

But I hope I've grown out of it.

Reminds me of an incident in the wardroom when I was stationed in the naval barracks in Chatham. Most of us midshipmen were training to become cypher officers, but there were two who weren't. They were *the* most frightful poseurs you could ever wish to meet – or rather, wish *not* to meet. They were always bragging to each other in loud voices about where they'd been or who they'd met – never about anything they'd actually *done*, which was what riled the rest of us. If they'd ever accomplished anything worth boasting about, we wouldn't have minded. Eventually one of them, propping up the bar with his friend, was heard to remark, 'Is that the fifteenth or sixteenth country we've visited?' in the sort of stage whisper people adopt when they're saying something for the benefit of everyone else within earshot, expecting to create an impression. It was one brag too often. One of our number rose from his chair with his glass of beer in his hand, walked up to the bar and emptied the contents over the bombastic little shyster's head and without saying a word returned to his chair.

There was absolute silence. Made the point for all of us, we thought.

But if that's what you do to the next saloon bar bore you run into swanking to the assembled company about how Barbados is *so* last year, don't try to blame me for putting the idea into your head if you end up getting a fourpenny one.

August 1956

POSTSCRIPT

He was so self-important that he wouldn't sit down in his own presence.

Goodnight.

E

EXETER

'Tis an ill clutch that blows nobody any good....

On Wednesday the men were coming to our flat in Dartmouth to install the rest of the double glazing, so on Tuesday we drove down.

At least, that was the plan. The Almighty had other ideas.

When we changed over drivers Margaret found the clutch beginning to slip. Yes, I'd noticed it, and was intending to take it in to my local garage next week and get it fixed. Unfortunately, I hadn't told the clutch that salvation was in the offing, and ten miles short of Honiton going up a hill just after some roadworks it burned out, choking the driver behind in black smoke. That's it. Call the AA.

Luckily we had lunch with us – sandwiches with the remains of last Sunday's joint – and had planned to stop as usual in a lay-by as the weather was decent for the time of year (mid-December). The AA promised to be with us within the hour, but in fact the patrolman turned up after forty minutes. No emergency repairs were possible – the smell was proof enough that the only 'repair' was a new clutch. So he hooked us up on a towbar and headed off to the AA's nominated garage in Exeter, twenty miles away. Requires enormous concentration being towed at speed along a motorway when all you can do is steer and try to keep directly behind the towing vehicle but with no control over anything else. Also has a tendency to render the trousers a bit damp.

Part of my deal with the AA is a free hire car in case of such an emergency, but the problem was that the garage was on one side of the city and the firm hiring the car on the other. Being on our way down for a stay of several days we had a bootful of luggage, all of which had to be unloaded and stacked however we could in the patrolman's vehicle, which wasn't designed for such a contingency. But we managed it, and jammed ourselves into the front seats of his van and took it in turns to breathe in. If Margaret and I hadn't been married, one of us would have been done for assault.

We'd been coming down to the West Country for many years, ever since, in fact, I first brought my then fiancée to visit her prospective mother-in-law in Dartmouth in 1958. We came to the river bank at the Higher Ferry on the opposite side of the town, saw it laid out before us in the sunshine and fell in love with it on sight. When our boys were small and money was tight we used to come down for long weekends B&B, and at a time when Humphrey liked to get up at some godforsaken hour in the morning we'd give him 50p the night before and instruct him to go to the newsagent just down the road and buy us our morning paper and bring it back at eight o'clock and not a moment earlier. We felt quite confident that an 8-year old wouldn't come to any harm alone on the streets of Dartmouth in the early morning, and he never did – even though when he'd bought the paper instead of coming straight back to our guest house he used to go down to the South Embankment and walk along the river and come back from the opposite direction. The 1970s were more innocent times. Not so sure I'd take the same view nowadays.

Another reason bringing us to the West Country over the years was that my mother remarried for a second time in Flavel Church

Exeter Quay   (photo: Exeter City Council)

in Dartmouth, moved from there to Totnes, then to near Newton Abbot, then to Foxholes near St Austell, then to Newlyn, then to Penzance and finally to Long Rock on the road to Marazion. We visited in school holidays, and often stopped off at Dartmouth on the way home to extend the break. In all those years, we always drove straight past Exeter on the A38 or by-passed it on the road across Dartmoor via Moretonhampstead and only once went into the city – to visit the cathedral.

So being now by happenstance in the city again, once we'd been deposited by the AA patrolman at the hire car firm and had picked up our temporary vehicle we thought it only made sense as we had time to spare to make the most of our chance visit and explore the city before heading on to Dartmouth. We found Exeter to be a quite delightful place, especially when we left the cathedral precinct and found our way down to the river where in the days when ships were a lot smaller they delivered goods to merchants and loaded cargo for shipment. We managed a short walk through the main shopping area, but by then it was time to go – we had to get to Dartmouth (not very far), but when we got there we had to unpack our stuff for the rest of our stay and do a bit of shopping for fresh supplies like, for example, tomorrow's breakfast.

*The Quay in Dartmouth. In the TV series 'The Onedin Line',
set in the mid-19th century, it stood in for Liverpool.*

There are pros and cons to having a second home, when you come to think about it. Before buying bricks and mortar we came to Dartmouth for a few days in a year, but then perhaps not again for several years afterwards. So walking around the picturesque old part of the town was always a delight, unsullied by over-familiarity. Once you buy, you feel under pressure to come down not just every year but every month to make sure you're getting your money's worth and at a more mundane level just to keep an eye on things and cut the grass, re-paint a wall, pick the post up off the doormat and so on.

After a few years, going down to your holiday home is no longer a holiday but a chore – you go because you have to, not because you particularly want to. Learning this lesson by experience, I always stood firm when Margaret wanted us to buy a place in France, where she very much enjoyed the lifestyle (as do I) and the cuisine. My objection was this: as things are, we can go to France four or five times a year (which we did right up to the time of her death), but always to different places to see new things, and as for those places we liked from previous visits we can always make a detour or just pop in for an overnight stay and have dinner in that nice restaurant or walk up that medieval cobbled street again or whatever. If we buy somewhere, then we'll have to go back to that same place every time and we'll lose our present freedom to explore all over – and added to that over time we'll get bored with the place because we'll have seen everything within range and there's nothing new left to do or see 'cos we've done it all and seen it all. Is that what you want? Answer: No. So we never did buy ourselves a *pied-à-terre*, and now that she's no longer here I'm glad I don't have the responsibility of managing a property on the other side of the Channel and having to make regular visits alone just to see that everything's alright. Keeping tabs on our flat in Dartmouth is difficult enough (a round trip of 300 miles), without having the added encumbrance of needing to book a ferry.

That's not to imply, let alone say, that I have any regrets about buying where we did. Anyone who knows Dartmouth knows that parking is difficult at any time, and impossible in the town in the summer. When we went house-hunting, we laid down three essential criteria: there had to be two bedrooms, so that we could go down with a friend if needs be, or lend the flat to friends with a child or friends who were not married to each other; it had to have a parking space of its own, not on the public highway, so that we could be sure that no matter at what time of the day or night we arrived we'd always have somewhere to park the car; and thirdly, it had to be walking distance from the town centre, so that once we'd arrived we could leave the car on site and not need it in order to get to the town itself.

Our choice fell on a basement flat which met our three demands, and we enjoyed many a short break over twenty years until finally deciding that we preferred exploring France and getting lost in the French countryside to retracing our steps month in and year out across Dartmoor – beautiful though that can be, especially in winter. When the suggestion across the breakfast table that 'it's time we went down to the flat' was met with a curl of the lip rather than a smile, I knew the time had come to re-think: sell up, or at least let it to a permanent resident. And so the situation remains. Between tenants we enjoyed some more short breaks, which were just like old times because we hadn't been for a couple of years and we thoroughly enjoyed reacquainting ourselves with restaurants, cafés and local shopkeepers we'd got to know over the years. The rental income paid for many a trip to France, so we had our holidays 'free' just as was the case – in pure economic terms – when we used to spend our holidays in our own (second) home.

So there you have it. A story which starts off about a chance mechanical breakdown leading to a revelatory visit to an ancient cathedral city, moves on to a few nuggets of folksy family history in historic Dartmouth and finally ends with some gentle philosophising on the subject of second homes.

And no doubt the local Tourist Boards will have no reason not to be pleased, either.

As a postscript, you may not have heard the following limerick, which was current during my student days and was regularly included in rugby club sing-songs:

> There was a young lady of Exeter,
> All the boys used to crane their neckseter.
> But one silly sod
> Got six months in quad
> For waving his organ of sexeter.

December 2005

POSTSCRIPT
Walking along a country road, I met a little farm girl, about 8 years old, leading an enormous bull.

Me: 'Hello, little girl. You're very small to be leading such a great big bull. Where are you going with him?'
Little girl: 'I'm taking him to a field so that he can make all the cows have calves.'
Me: 'Can't you father do it?'
Little girl: 'No, only the bull.'

Goodnight.

F

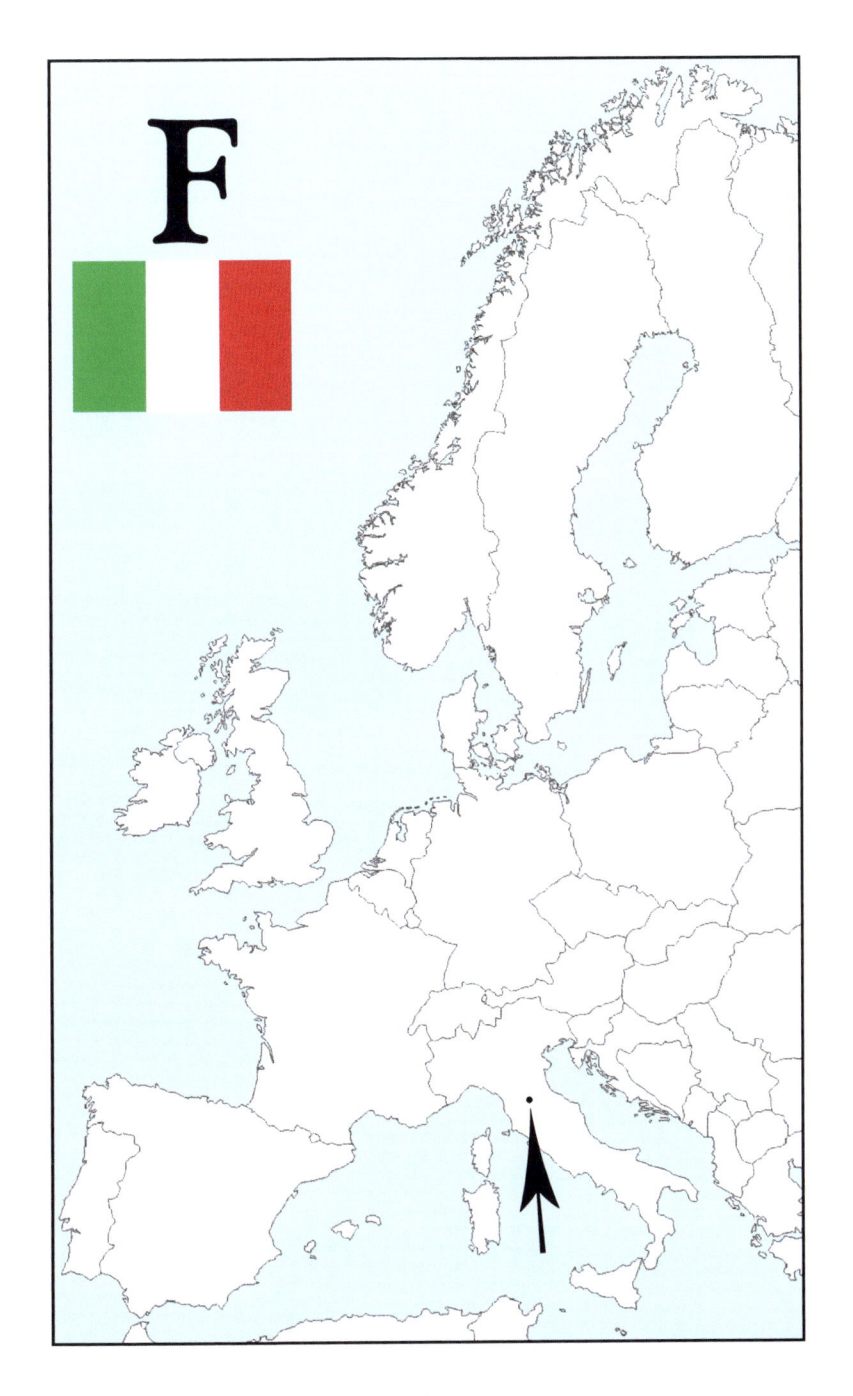

FIORENZA

FIRENZE

Returning to normal

Brunelleschi's famous Dome was completed in 1436.

When you're mayor of the borough, for one whole year someone always opens the door for you, you enter every room first, everyone stands up, you get first pick of the buffet and your coffee's hot when they serve it. Well, there's a lot more to it than that, but you get the idea.

But it means that for that year you are *Numero Uno*, until your year is up and you pass the chain of office over to your successor. From being 'Madame Mayor' one day – I'm talking about Margaret, not me – the next morning you're back to 'Who?' and 'How do you spell your name?'. It can be quite a shock to the system. Moral: enjoy it while it lasts, but remember the bowing and scraping is to you as the office-holder, not to you as a person.

We decided that the way to smooth the transition from First Citizen back to normal life was to get right away for a week as soon as possible after the end of Margaret's mayoral year, and take a holiday somewhere a bit exotic. We'd both long wanted to visit Florence, so that's what we did.

And who should be on the plane but our MP, Sir David Price,

and his wife – on last because of her need for wheelchair space. The significance of his appearance on this flight becomes apparent when I explain that at the general election two years before I'd been one of his opponents, so we'd been acquainted for a long time. Contrary to most people's presumptions about politicians in opposing parties, we had a high degree of mutual respect and got on quite well when we met at functions. But I did remark to Margaret that perhaps he was just making sure that he wouldn't have to face me at an election again as I was leaving the country and, this being Italy, just to make sure he'd been in touch with his local friends in *Cosa Nostra* and was coming in person to make sure his instructions were carried out. . .

It struck us as strange that a major city such as Florence didn't have its own airport – you flew to Pisa and took the train. But we settled into our hotel in the suburbs (couldn't afford city centre accommodation) and travelled in by bus every day to visit the historic sites. The mayoral year had been very strenuous, and what we really wanted was a good rest and some gentle sight-seeing without having either to rush around to some tour guide's schedule or worry about which side of the road to drive on. That's why we travelled by public transport, and independently instead of taking a package tour.

Being myself well versed in European history I was able to really enjoy seeing so many buildings which I had read about or seen in pictures. Having lunch in a beautiful square, I shuddered slightly to recall that Savonarola had been burned alive for heresy outside the building opposite – the same building, it was still there – and imagined what the crowd scene would have been like back in 1498, in contrast to the ambience we were enjoying sitting in the sunshine over a meal and a bottle of wine without a care in the world. In Rouen one of our favourite restaurants for lunch is Les Maraîchers, just across the road from the site where Joan of Arc was burned at the stake – in this case only memorials and plaques mark the spot, as Second World War bombs destroyed the originals.

Copy of Michelangelo's David in the Palazzo Vecchio

Two doors away is *La Couronne*, which claims to have records going back to 1345 and so to be the oldest restaurant in France. This means that if you have a sufficiently sick sense of humour you can imagine yourself (or maybe one of your ancestors – who knows, one of them might have been there at the time) sitting in that very tavern on 29 May 1431 watching the sweating English soldiery arranging the faggots around *La Pucelle* and the executioner lighting his torch in readiness while you stick your knife into a meat pie and shout at the pot boy to bring you another tankard – 'Hurry up! Those flames are going to be really, really hot when they barbecue the witch and the thought's making me thirsty!'. As I said, you have to have a sufficiently sick sense of humour...By way of an expiative palliative, let me offer you this one: in a medieval recipe for thick broth there appears the instruction: '*When the cauldron is boiling fiercely, pop in a scullion*'.

The Ponte Vecchio dates from 1345, when it replaced an earlier bridge destroyed by floods.

But it's not unusual for tourists who visit sites of historical interest to find themselves at some location where centuries ago scenes of unspeakable horror took place, yet here you are as a tourist relaxing and drinking coffee as though nothing had ever happened and the locals are just getting on with their everyday lives – serving the said coffee, selling papers, having lunch, going to the hairdresser's, meeting a date, pushing a pram or buying new shoes for the kids. If you've ever, for example, walked amongst the ruins of Pompeii, you'll know what I mean. However tranquil it looks now, it was a bit different on 24 August 79 AD.

Like all tourists, we visited the Uffizi Gallery, the Boboli Gardens and Fiesole and one day took the train to Pisa for the Leaning Tower, which was open to the public so we were allowed to go up the spiral staircase inside. To get a view of the ground on the lower side, during the ascent I took my life in my hands by walking through one of the ornamental archways onto the exterior parapet. There was nothing to hold on to and all that kept me in position was the friction

Leaning Tower of Pisa
photo: Wikimedia

of the soles of my shoes on the stone as I leaned back against the wall with arms outstretched on either side while peering at the ground some fifty feet below.

I'm actually quite scared of heights, and when we got to the top found that the only security was an iron rail on uprights about four feet high. I gripped this very tightly, and when Margaret took a photo she said she could distinctly see the yellow streak running down my back because the truth was I was scared stiff! There was a fine view looking down onto the roof of the adjcent cathedral, but it wasn't good for the nerves.

Then to the cathedral, where at the entrance a bouncer with an oversized belly kept intoning 'No shorts' at anyone so dressed, which was, I surmised, the only English he knew. To this day, why the Almighty would be offended by a tourist visiting his place of worship in shorts escapes me.

We had one nasty moment during our stay. I was strap-hanging in the bus into town when I happened to catch sight of the headline in the paper over another passenger's shoulder. The only Italian I knew was through singing Verdi and Puccini in my student days in the Operatic Society, but I could just make out that there'd been some disaster in Belgium, with pictures of a sports stadium and numbers of dead and injured and comments about English football hooligans. I suddenly twigged: it was the match between Liverpool and Juventus at the Heysel Stadium in Brussels, and something terrible had happened and the Brits were to blame. My immediate thought was: 'What's happened, and will we be at risk here in Italy because the moment we open our mouths it's obvious that we're English?'

As I couldn't be sure I'd read the story properly we decided to minimise our risks and head back to the safety of our hotel and ask the receptionist to explain. He told us that English football supporters had attacked Italian fans and numerous deaths had resulted. I asked him straight:

'Is it safe for us on the streets of Florence?'.

He was reassuring.

'Of course you are. It wasn't you!'

'Maybe so, but we're English and if someone here's lost his cousin because of English hooligans and he wants revenge or just to vent his anger, any English person will do.'

'No worries. We Florentines aren't like that.'

As it turned out, he was right. We encountered no hostility whatever.

I recalled this episode some years later, when staying in a pub in the far south-west of Ireland. One day while we were there news came through of an IRA bomb attack in the North, where a bus carrying British soldiers had been blown up and eight of them killed. Our landlord and all his customers went out of their way to assure us that it had nothing to do with them and they didn't support the IRA, let alone condone atrocities. As one of them put it: 'We don't want the North anyway. It's as much as our government can manage to look after the eighteen counties we've already got, without adding another six!'

At the end of our lovely week, steeped in history, art and Italian wine, we took the train back to Pisa and got on the plane home. And who was on it too? Believe it or not – Sir David and his wife.

May 1985

POSTSCRIPT

First man: 'I hear the chap who bought the Big House at auction spent a small fortune on renovating it and now he's homeless and gone back to London to live. Why's that?'

Second man: 'Last spring he added new east wing and in the summer he built a new west wing. With two new wings, when autumn came the house flew away.'

Goodnight.

G

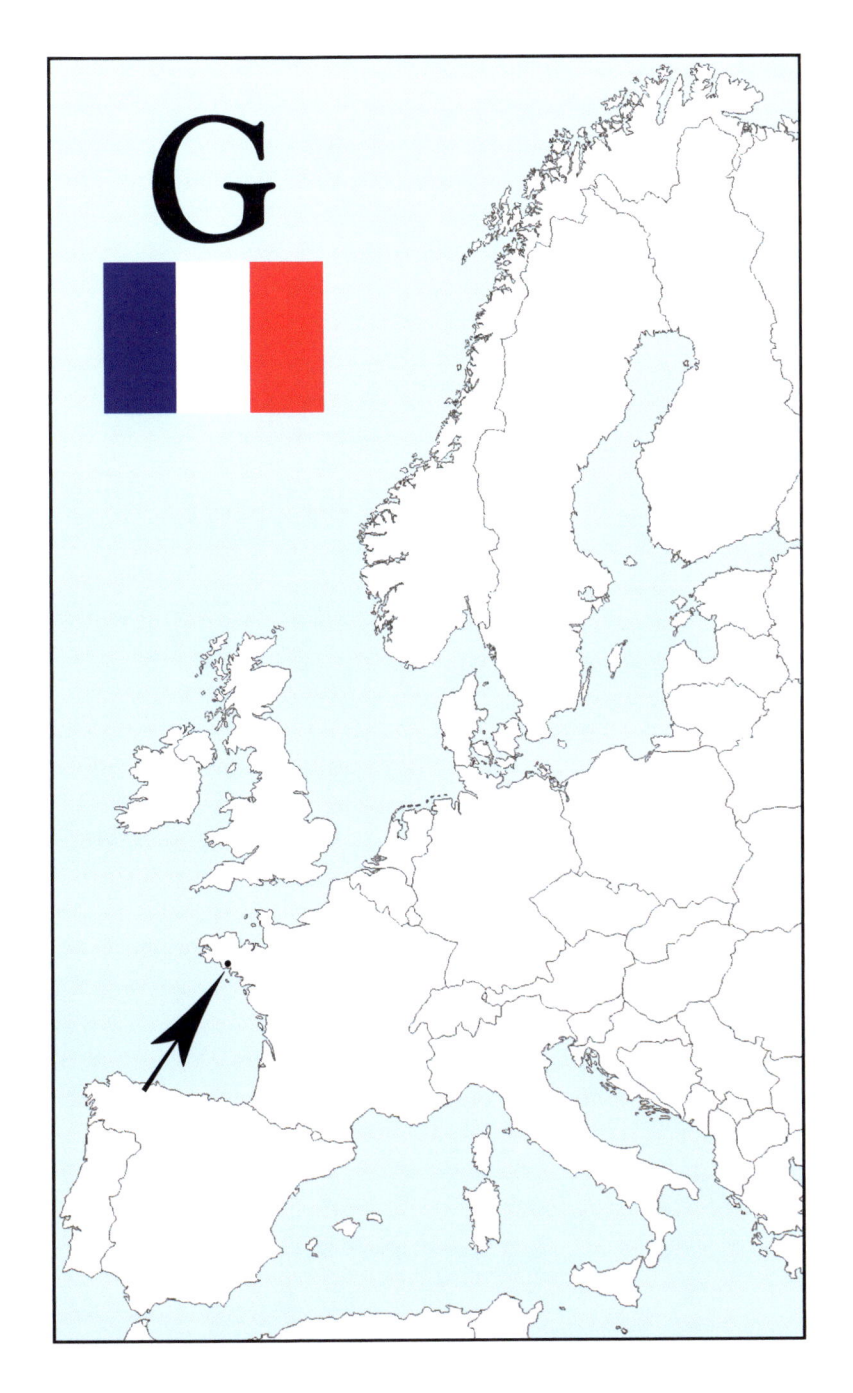

GAVRINIS

Stone me!

Margaret had always wanted to take a proper look at Carnac, one of the largest neolithic sites in the world with dead straight lines of standing stones stretching over a kilometre. The town is divided into two distinct areas, a couple of kilometres apart: Carnac proper and the seaside resort of Carnac-Plage, which is full of cafés, restaurants, hotels and holidaymakers and their children (the beaches are excellent, so no wonder!). But in our opinion 'old' Carnac boasted some rather more interesting restaurants, and whenever possible we opted to make the short drive up the hill to eat there. It also has an interesting church, with a statue on an outside wall of St Cornelius, Pope 251-3, who according to legend fled persecution under Emperor Trebonianus Gallus *(no – I'd never heard of him either)* and was pursued to Brittany, where the Roman soldiers chasing him were turned into stones and that accounts for the lines of standing stones to be found outside Carnac... Legend is a wonderful thing!

We'd rented a *gîte* in Carnac-Plage for convenience, as a central point to explore the area, but had considerable trouble finding it when we arrived because the street nameplate was not on the side of the road facing us as we approached but on the opposite side – which meant we only found it when, having got lost, we turned round and came back. Added to which, our little road was a cul-de-sac, so no way in from the other end so therefore no nameplates. The *gîte* was comfortably furnished and we thought we were in for a relaxing stay, until we tried to use the shower and the tap wouldn't budge, leaving us with the dilemma: do you increase the amount of force and risk breaking the tap and flooding the bathroom, or do you forego showers and just wash down using the washbasin? Not what you expect when you've paid top dollar for a house for a week in high summer. Things reached their nadir when the night before we were due to leave the lock in the front door jammed and we could only get out of the house by climbing through a window.

As is our wont, we sought out the local 'little train' and took a tour of the area. The Carnac-Plage version takes passengers for a joy-ride along the coast through the town and on to other nearby resorts, and then veers off into the countryside along the road which runs parallel to the neolithic site, giving passengers an excellent view of its entire length. Next day we went back in the car so that we could wander amongst the stones and read the guidebook and the helpful information panels erected by the local authorities.

Margaret's wishes now having been satisfied, it was my turn. My light-hearted goal of visiting every island off the French coast accessible by a public ferry turns up some difficult destinations. Gavrinis is one such.

Off the French coast it may be, but it's not in the sea but in the virtually land-locked Gulf of Morbihan. So small you wouldn't notice it on an ordinary map, the fact that it's the location of the highest neolithic tumulus in the whole of Brittany means it's highlighted on all the appropriate tourist brochures.

The problem is: how to get there.

It's only about twenty kilometres west of Vannes as the crow flies, but with such an indented coastline it's double that in road mileage (or should that be "kilometrage"?). You'd expect the principal ferry to the island to start out from Vannes, as the main centre for visitors, tourists, archaeology groupies and, as it's also the capital of that part of Brittany, where there is the greatest concentration of hotels.

Vannes is the starting point for many ferries, in particular for the "real" ones serving the ordinary residents on the two islands in the Gulf which are not in private hands, namely the Ile d'Arz and the Ile aux Moines, which need a regular commercial ferry to get to the mainland for shopping, private business (seeing their dentist, perhaps?) in the same way that the rest of us might need a bus to the local supermarket or a train service to go to a theatre in the next town. But not for Gavrinis, oh no!

There are two possibilities. One is from Port Navalo, on the tip of the Presqu'île de Rhuys and an hour's circuitous drive from Vannes, and when you get there you'd be doubling back on yourself. The other is from Locmariaquer, on the opposite side of the Gulf. But that's a small place well off the main road north-west of Vannes, and also at the end of yet another peninsula so on the way to nowhere. In other words, you wouldn't be going there by car *en route* for anywhere else. If you went there, it would be for a purpose.

Well, of course, we *had* a purpose: to catch the ferry to Gavrinis – what else?

Ferry? Well, I suppose so. Room for a couple of dozen passengers in comfort – but possibly that reflects the number of passengers who normally want to cross the mouth of the Gulf to get to Port Navalo. It took fifteen minutes or so, then fresh passengers embarked for the journey up to the top of the Gulf to deposit us all on Gavrinis.

We were blessed with a calm day, bright sunshine and perfect visibility. The Gulf is dotted with islands, most very small and often tree-covered or if privately owned featuring a single house and a rudimentary landing stage. But with no commercial traffic it was very relaxing. On our approach to Gavrinis we passed near another archaeological curiosity: an adjacent islet with a set of stones running from dry land into the water which are partly submerged at high tide. Students and enthusiasts occasionally visit it, but we had a perfect view and could take pictures from various angles – enough to satisfy any non-specialist tourist.

Being a monument of major importance, Gavrinis itself boasts a proper jetty and a stout iron fence surrounds the tumulus to prevent unauthorised or unaccompanied visitors. Public access is through a locked gate – open only during visiting hours. Guided tours only, to protect such a unique and valuable site. But the detailed illustrative panels carry explanations only in French. Well, this is France – but how many tourists have a working knowledge of archaeological terms in a language other than their own? Many of the specialist words are not found even in a standard dictionary, let alone in the pocket variety a tourist might be carrying. A site of international importance should, surely, also allow for the probability that some visitors – even experts or specialists – have only a limited command of French. I've encountered similar obstacles elsewhere and at other times – as, probably, have you.

Not that we in England are any better in facilitating understanding of historic sites for foreign visitors by helping out with a glossary of terms for those whose English may be good enough for ordinary business – travelling around, booking hotels, enquiring about bus tickets, shopping or eating out – but who may not know the words 'keep', 'moat' or 'drawbridge'. If they're francophone they may think that the English word 'dungeon' means the same as French 'donjon' (which actually *is* a keep), whereas in reality our similar-sounding word is totally misleading because it refers to something which could be fifty (vertical) metres wide of the mark, if you follow.

The tumulus on Gavrinis has been dated by experts to $c3700$BC and was abandoned, they tell us, around 3000BC. It consists of a dolmen covered by a cairn of stones, the entrance to which was not discovered until the first serious excavation was undertaken in 1835. The mound of stones has a diameter of about 50m and in modern times a padlocked door has been added which helps protect the interior from the weather and also prevents unauthorised entry. A passage 14m long, a metre or so wide and between 1½m and 2m high leads to a chamber 2½m square. By the light of the guide's torch the side walls, which consist of a continuous line of enormous granite boulders, can be seen to be entirely incised with typical neolithic patterns of concentric circles, axes and what experts say may be representations of animals and gods. No one knows for sure. One's ability to see the carvings is not helped by the corridor being packed, as the guide takes in about two dozen people at a time.

A question every visitor has in his mind is that the granite blocks weigh many tonnes so how on earth did our neolithic ancestors transport them to an island? The truth is, Gavrinis wasn't an island when the dolmen was built because the water level in the Gulf was some 15m lower. Even then, the questions remain: how did they manage to dig up such enormous blocks and transport them, and the other unanswered question: why? Comparisons with Stonehenge come to mind: how and why? And what sort of society was it that thought such tremendous effort was worth it and persisted over centuries?

Recreactions of dug-out canoes

May 2010

POSTSCRIPT
'*Primus inter pares*'. We're camping under the Eiffel Tower.

H

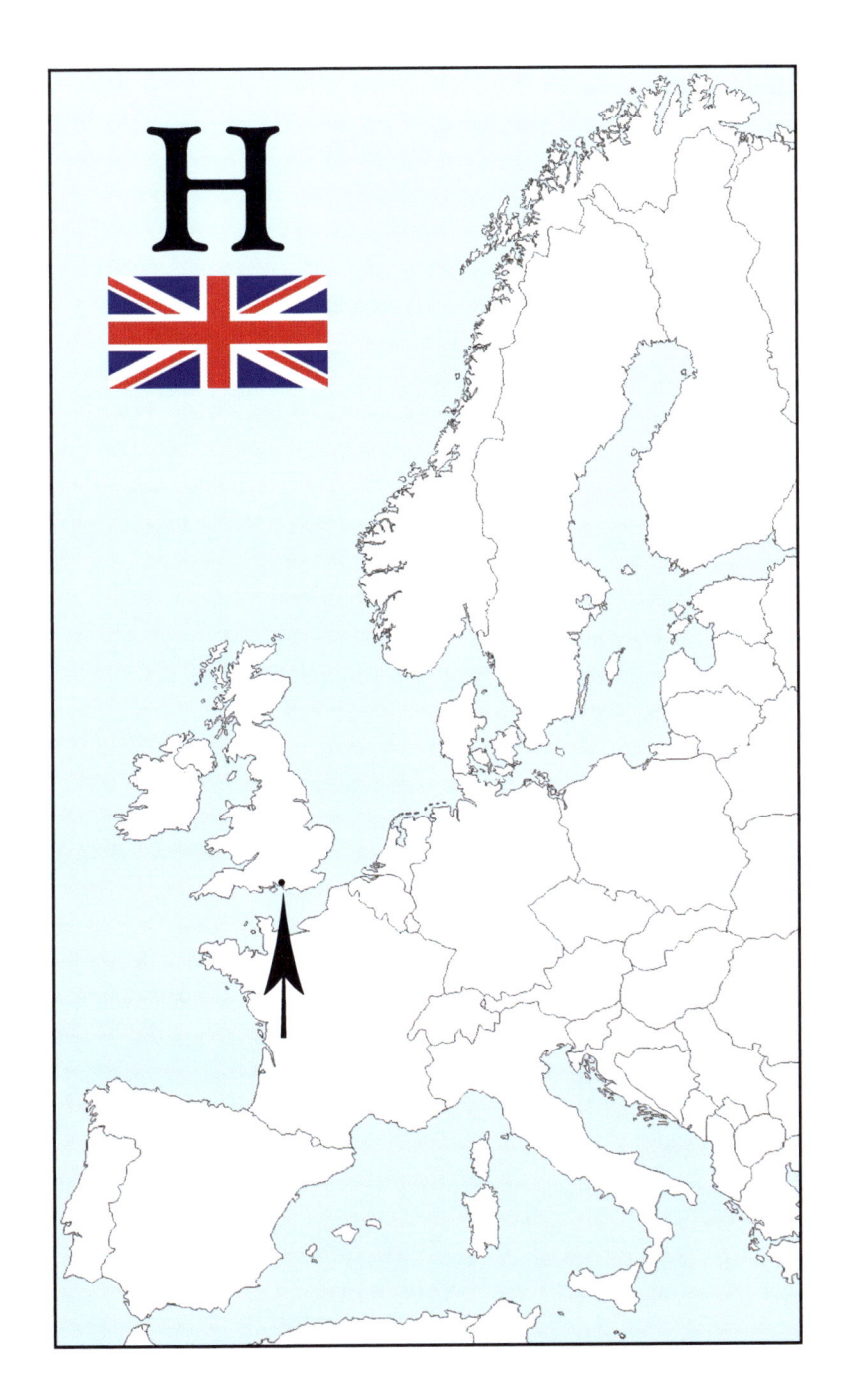

HORNDEAN

'The Good Old Days' – or were they?

When I was a schoolboy one of the ways us lads could make a bit of cash to supplement our pocket-money (assuming we got any) was to work for the local farmers in early autumn 'stooking', i.e. going out into the fields and walking behind the harvester and picking up a sheaf of corn in each hand and banging the tops together and then two more and so on to make a 'stook' consisting of six sheaves. Then move on and build another stook. All day long. Damned hard work, in the broiling sun and your forearms covered in pin-pricks from the cut ends of the corn. I think our pay was 1s 3d an hour (yes – 6p in our money, but the cost of living was entirely different in those days).

The other way to get hold of some extra funds was to work on the Post Office at Christmas.

Horndean Post Office was also a general store, with the proprietor's name over the doorway: 'B.J. BISH'. As postmaster, Mr Bish took me on as a 'temp' at 15, without seeming to bother about regulations which I think stipulated a minimum age of 16. He signed me on again the following year and in fact every year until I left school. I think he was glad to be able to take on a grammar school boy who could read and who, living in Clanfield on the outer reaches of his area, knew all the by-ways and lanes leading to outlying cottages and farms and who could therefore be relied upon to deliver their post.

I had to sign on by 6 a.m., which meant cycling from my home, a distance of a couple of miles. We started in the sorting office at the back of the premises, where I helped the regular postmen sort the incoming mail and put it into rounds. When this was complete I went out on a post office bike carrying the additional mail with one of the 'regulars', delivering to my own village and the surrounding farms. We did everything by bike – wind, rain or snow notwithstanding – and as this was in the middle of the South Downs we had some pretty demanding hills. They may not be very high, but they are often very steep.

I remember Horndean from a much earlier age than 15, from five in fact. When I reached that age and had to go to school, for some reason my grandparents who were bringing me up sent me to school in Blendworth, half a mile up the hill from Horndean, instead of to the village school in Clanfield. This meant that between the ages of five and eight I walked half a mile from my home up to the main A3 to catch the bus, went three stops to Horndean, got off and walked up the hill to the school in Blendworth and then repeated the journey at the end of the school day. Starting as an unaccompanied five-year old, remember, carrying my satchel with books, pens etc. and in all weathers.

Blendworth School was a single-storey building with a two-storey house attached, where Mrs Byrne, the head teacher, lived. There were two classrooms. Miss Miller, on the upper edge of middle age, took the five- to seven-year olds in one room, Mrs Byrne took the rest in the other. We sat two to a double desk, which had a bench seat attached on a black iron frame and holes for two inkwells and a groove for pens and pencils when not in use. The sloping top was hinged and when lifted revealed a space to store books and one's sandwiches for lunch (there was no school kitchen, nor any provision for hot food or drink). The desks stood in rows going back five deep to the rear wall, with two rows making up a 'standard', i.e. an age group. So Standard 4 was the two rows on the teacher's left, who'd be eight-year olds. Next to them and directly in front of Mrs Byrne were two rows of nine-year olds, and then on her right the top Standard, those in their final year before going on to secondary school. The three classes would all be doing different subjects, so Mrs Byrne might be teaching Standard 4 English, i.e. how to write and spell, Standard 6 might be having a history lesson, and sitting between the two would be Standard 5 doing nature study – all at the same time and in the same room and with just one teacher.

Our playground was a tarmac area bounded by a low fence of rounded iron railings facing the road and painted black, then at right angles a flint wall on the other side of which was the churchyard.

At the far end was the boys' urinal, consisting of a three-sided brick construction with the back wall and trough sealed with bitumen and open to the sky. Why Nan – my grandmother – chose to send me here – two half-mile walks and a bus fare – instead of to the much nearer village school in Clanfield – a mile-and-a-half across the fields, and no bus fare – I never found out, but as it turned out she withdrew me when I was eight and sent me to Clanfield School instead.

Back to Horndean. After we'd completed our morning round – usually not before two o'clock – we returned to sort mail for the afternoon shift. As well as two deliveries a day we even did a complete round on Christmas morning (for double time, so well worth it) and I got home for my Xmas Dinner at about two o'clock, having been up since five. We had a van for parcels, and my particular pleasure was to be assigned to this duty as that meant I had to knock on people's doors to deliver their parcel and if it had some interesting stamps on it I could ask if I could have them for my collection. Usually people were quite happy to give me the stamps, which otherwise they'd have thrown away, especially if it was a bitterly cold day and they took pity on the snow-covered post boy standing at their door in a howling gale. Some would tear them off there and then and give them to me, others would tell me to collect them next time I called. I built up quite a tidy collection that year! A lot of the stamps I got were, of course, from neighbours or other people living in the village whom I knew. Some of them, knowing that I was interested, kept their stamps for me long after I'd stopped being a 'temp' postie and would call me over when I was riding my bike along the lane or if they met me in the shop buying the weekly groceries for Nan and tell me they'd got some more stamps for me and to pop in and collect them. I sometimes got a cup of tea as well, or in hot weather a glass of lemonade. And sometimes an errand to run – e.g. post the reply to the letter from the country from which the stamps had come that I'd just been given. Seemed the least I could do – especially as the outcome would probably be another batch of stamps.

Harry, one of the regular postmen, had a specially adapted bike.

One pedal was fixed at full stretch for his foot to rest on and didn't go round, leaving his other leg to do all the pedalling. He'd been injured in the War (the First one, of course), and had an artificial leg but no control over the knee movement so could power the wheels on his bike only with his good leg. Despite all the hills, he seemed to manage them on his one-legged bike. At least he could always be absolutely sure that no one else would take it!

A last word about Horndean. During the two months of low temperatures and high snowfall we had no buses for six weeks and if I wanted to get to school at Purbrook, seven miles away, the buses which normally ran from Portsmouth to Petersfield could only get that far, and I had to walk to Horndean in the morning – hoping there'd be a bus to Purbrook – and then in the afternoon the reverse walk – about two miles – home. I had to try to get to school regardless of the weather conditions, as I was due to sit for my school certificate in the summer and one's entire future depended on success in that examination.

December 1948

POSTSCRIPT
Anyone wanting to make stamp collecting illegal could write to the papers calling for philately to be stamped out.

Goodnight.

I

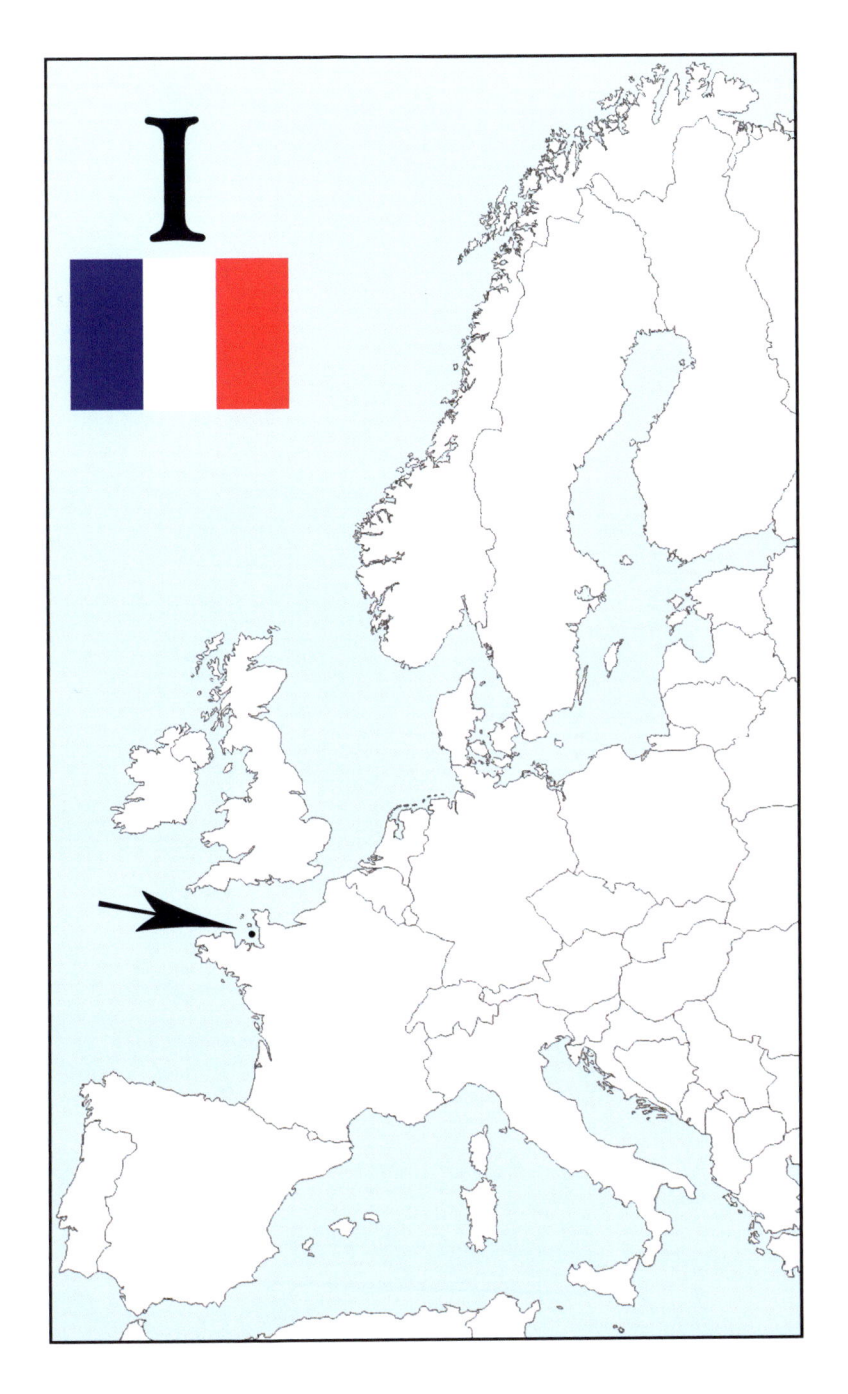

ÎLES CHAUSEY

An island life that is no longer
[Conversations in italics were in French]

Most people think of the Channel Islands as being 'ours', i.e. part of the United Kingdom. Say that to a Channel Islander and s/he'll jump on you straight away and point out that as the last surviving relic of the Duchy of Normandy whose Duke, William, conquered England in 1066 it's actually the other way round. They're not part of us, we're part of them. They are subject to the English crown as the Queen is the lawful successor to the dukes of Normandy, but absolutely *not* subject to the English Parliament. Jersey and Guernsey have their own parliaments, stamps and coins to prove it.

But to the south there's another cluster of islands in the Channel which are part of France: Chausey and the surrounding rocky islets. Not many people know that, as they say. Officially there are 52 of them, but with a difference between high and low tide of 14m (about 45 feet in old money) many are submerged at high water, so it depends when you count them; allegedly there are 365 at low tide – one for each day of the year. From Granville the main island is visible some 17km distant on the horizon, and has a lighthouse (now automated – the last lighthousemen left in 2008) and a hotel, a restaurant and a café all open to visitors in the summer months. In the old days the islanders scraped a living by keeping a few sheep, harvesting seaweed and fishing – especially for lobsters. But the island priest locked the chapel for the last time and moved to the mainland in the 1970s and practically everyone else followed him a decade later, as these activities no longer provided a decent living. The little island school was abandoned and the workers' cottages sold off as holiday homes. Out of season the island retains only about thirty inhabitants, most of them maintenance staff. Elsewhere away from the landing stage there are a couple of private residences visible to passers-by through ornate gates at the end of long drives. However, these gates don't appear to be attached to completed walls, so more for appearance than security.

At low tide there are innumerable sandy beaches, rocky coves and delightful views over jagged rocks, but when the tide comes in you need to grab your clothes and picnic gear and leg it to above high water mark otherwise you will be caught out by the precipitate and unexpected speed at which the water comes up the beach.

It was the last weekend before the season ended, so as soon as we'd settled into our hotel in Granville I headed down to the ticket office in the harbour to make sure we were safely booked on the boat the following morning. I didn't want us to turn up and find it was full. As it happened, several hundred French holidaymakers seemed to have had the same idea because the weather forecast was bright sunshine, and altogether three boats laden with day-trippers made the crossing that day. But we were the only foreigners, and in fact I've never met any other English person who's been there. The voyage takes fifty minutes. The boats dropped everyone off and then tied up in the bay until five o'clock, when everyone clambered back for the return run. Being a crew member sounded like a real doddle.

Like a lot of others, our first thought on landing was refreshment. At the top of the slipway was the café and behind it the restaurant, so we headed for the one farther away as possibly likely to be less crowded. While ordering coffee I noticed the word *homard* scrawled in chalk on a little blackboard hanging beside the door to the kitchen. And at a knock-down price – about a quarter of what you'd expect to pay normally.

Now there's a thought . . .

'Is that available today?' I asked the chap behind the counter.

'Yes. Caught this morning. They're in the tank in the kitchen. Choose the one you want.'

I'm not inordinately fond of lobster, but this seemed too good an opportunity to miss. I'll see what Margaret thinks.

'Do you fancy a fresh lobster for lunch? It's only thirteen quid for the two of us.'

'OK. Why not? It'll make a change.'

I beckoned.

'Come and choose.' I didn't mention that they were still . . .
'Oh! no! It's alive!'
'Yes. I said they were fresh. Now which one do you want?'

It feels a bit mean to point at a poor old lobster in a tank, claws tied together with red string, and condemn him to death just to grace your plate. But if we didn't eat him someone else would, as there weren't very many *homards* in the tank and there were a lot of customers behind me in the queue.

Grillé mayonnaise, he was very tasty!

We set off along the path leading to the far end of the island, but it twisted and meandered and the time required turned out to be a lot longer than we'd expected. However, we'd out-walked every other tripper off the boats, so as we were likely to be able to have the beach to ourselves wherever we stopped there seemed little point in walking farther just for the sake of it. We chose a lovely little bay with fine sand, piled our clothes and baggage above the high water mark and made our way down for a bathe. The water was hardly deep enough to swim in, as the slope of the beach was so gentle. But then I'm not much of a swimmer, and this dip at the end of September was the only time all that year that I went in the water.

When the tide turned we moved back without hanging

about; like the wise virgins we were, being on the lookout for this phenomenon and aware that getting caught might be mildly funny if all that happened was that you got your belongings wet but could be rather more serious if you got cut off. There were no lifeguards, and although there was a lifebelt on a stand at the top of the beach that's not going to be a lot of use if there's no one there to throw it to you. Visitors were warned by notices at the landing stage that the incoming tide could be dangerous, and to take note and not put themselves at risk.

We were disappointed to find the disused chapel locked, as we'd expected it to be opened on days when there would be visitors. The same with the schoolroom. A small terrace of workers' cottages, now private holiday homes, also seemed to be unoccupied and locked, which was a shame because we'd have liked to see the domestic arrangements of the former inhabitants and try to imagine what life must have been like for them. *[Memo to the Tourist Board: why not open one cottage and furnish it 'as was' so that visitors can enjoy a look at a time capsule?].* We resisted the temptation to venture onto private property and peer through the windows, just in case they *were* occupied and it was just a case of the owners not leaving the front door open because they were enjoying an afternoon snooze. Or they were – well, you can imagine what else they might be doing on a balmy afternoon on holiday, without me spelling it out in words of one syllable.

It's quite hard to conjure up a picture of life in centuries past for people struggling against the odds living and working, marrying and dying on such a tiny island within sight of the mainland. But the story of Chausey was explained on boards put up near the slipway, which is how we learned that it was still inhabited for a generation after the war and not finally abandoned until the 1980s. Life must have been harsh in winter; little of the land seemed to be much above sea level, and one could imagine during mid-winter gales the spray blowing across from one side of the island to the other. On a beautiful sunny day in late summer, though, it was ideal for a family day out with the kids. Many of our fellow trippers had not gone exploring but had passed their time sitting around near the café and

looking at the private boats moored all around the slipway.
Lazy days in the sun.

September 1999

POSTSCRIPT

When as a baby he was about to be christened, Jean-Paul Dupont bit the priest, who exclaimed *'Formidable!'* then gabbled 'Jean-Paul'. As a result, he was officially christened *'Formidable Jean-Paul Dupont.'* Throughout his life he found this a source of embarrassment, but his wife admitted that one of the things which originally attracted her to him was that she loved the idea of being married to a man named *Formidable*.

When in old age he approached death, he got her to promise not to put his official first name on his headstone – just Jean-Paul. She reluctantly agreed.

However, she was determined that despite this promise he would be remembered by his first name even though he'd hated it.

She inscribed his headstone: Here lies Jean-Paul Dupont, who satisfied his wife every night and never told her a lie.

Now whenever two Frenchmen pass by and read his headstone, one turns to the other and says *'Uh. Regardez-là. C'est formidable!'*.

Goodnight.

J

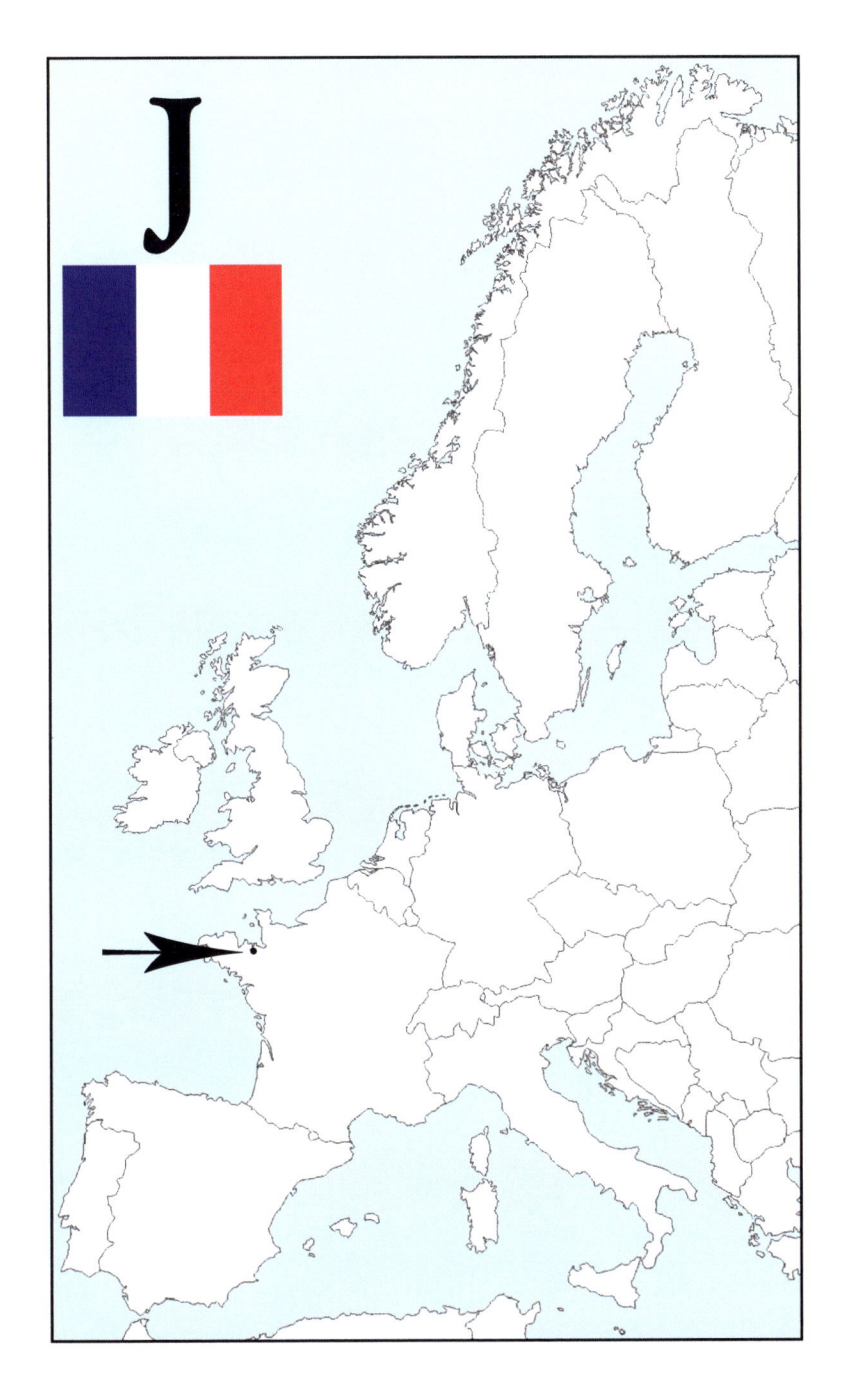

THE JERZUAL

[Conversations in italics were in French]

That's pretty steep!

The Jerzual is the cobbled road in Dinan up which goods were transported in the Middle Ages half a kilometre from the river to the town, and which has been preserved much as it was – retaining as well its challenging gradient at certain points of between 1:3 and 1:4. It's a real physical struggle to walk up from the port to the Old Town when it's dry underfoot, highly problematic when the cobbles are wet. On one occasion returning to our hotel after dinner in a restaurant down by the river my umbrella blew inside out! Thankfully, there are stone benches randomly situated on which to catch your breath, or wait for your partner to catch up.

One of my favourite holiday destinations, Dinan was from the 13th century onwards heavily fortified by the dukes of Brittany and still retains many of its original medieval buildings as well as the bulk of its defensive walls, with their associated towers and gateways. It claims to have the highest number of *'maisons à porche'* in France – houses whose upper storeys overhang the ground floor and are supported on massive wooden pillars. It fell into economic decline in the 18th and 19th centuries. Modernisation and redevelopment didn't take place simply because in the absence of much commercial activity no one could see any profit.

This wonderfully preserved historic gem is usually awash with tourists, especially from Britain. But how we first discovered it was most odd.

The belfry dates from the 15th century and is open to the public.

If you've read the first book in this series, my *Little Green Nightbook*, you may remember me telling you that I had a friend, Claude, whose way of thanking me for helping him win a seat on the county council (I was his election agent) was to offer us the use of his flat at Ouistreham on the coast of Normandy for a free holiday. We started by exploring the countryside round about, then the nearby metropolis of Caen, then ventured farther afield to Bayeux and Arromanches and the various beaches where the D-day landings took place in June 1944. Eventually, after a couple of years of holidays based on Claude's flat, we ran out of nearby places to visit which we hadn't been to before and needed to be a bit more adventurous and spread our net.

One day we set out with the intention of going as far west as we could while still leaving ourselves time to get back in daylight (I don't like driving at night on the 'wrong' side of the road). We ended up crossing the border into Brittany, and came to a fork in the road. (You mean a family staying at a campsite had dropped some cutlery? No. The other sort of fork – silly!). To the right, Dinard. To the left, Dinan. They sound much the same to an unattuned foreign ear. 'One of these is a seaside resort full of yachties', I said to Margaret. 'The other one is a medieval town which I've read about in tourist brochures'. But I can't remember which is which!' We plumped to go left.

As we drove up the main road into the vast market square in the heart of the town – the *Place du Guesclin* – I exclaimed to Margaret with an air of triumph 'This is it! This is the one we want.' We parked, had a quick look round and headed back to Ouistreham while the light held. But having seen Dinan, we were hooked and knew we'd be back. And we were – we came back time and again for twenty years!

The original town sits on a bluff above the River Rance, and was encircled by a massive defensive wall with towers and gates. These are still much in evidence, and permit the city to stage – in alternate years ending with even numbers – a medieval festival, the *Fête des Remparts*, over a weekend in July. Costumed townsfolk saunter through the streets, many shopkeepers don fifteenth century attire and itinerant tradesmen, jugglers, beggars and lepers lurk in alleyways and men-at-arms camped out below the walls engage in hand-to-hand combat or re-enact a medieval siege. Behind the basilica of Saint Sauveur lies a small park – le Jardin des Anglais

– where there's enough space to set up a camp and dedicate it to demonstrating some chosen aspect of medieval life. At the fête one year, for example, the chosen theme was 'Construction in the Middle Ages', i.e. how a cathedral was built, what instruments an architect would have employed and demonstrations of cutting stone and timber with medieval tools. At the next fête the theme was how justice worked; on another occasion it was 'Medicine in the Middle Ages'. I know, because we visited each time and saw what was going on.

The *pièce de résistance* of the *Fête des Remparts* is the jousting, which takes place in a sanded arena between the two largest round towers, some 40m high and in one of which the museum is housed. Tiers of seats are erected facing the curtain wall (€10 each) and right in the middle is a 10m high double doorway which following announcements by the Master of Ceremonies and a fanfare of trumpets is opened for the knights – usually six in number, with their squires and ostlers on foot carrying additional gear – to emerge mounted on their destriers, fully accoutred in plate armour and chain mail and armed with fifteenth century weapons, to be greeted by roars of welcome from loyal supporters in the crowd. My own initial reaction the first time I witnessed this carefully stage-managed spectacle was to wonder how the men facing them for real in a battle must have felt, seeing the enemy at full gallop coming to get them with swords, lances and mace-and-chain – all designed to rip you in half or smash your skull in. They must have been absolutely terrified! The origin, I suppose, of the modern phrase describing such a situation: 'shit scared'.

About two-thirds of the way up to the town the Jerzual passes through the original fortified gateway, Le Petit Port, and one year in order to attend the *Fête* we rented a *gîte* located upstairs in a building only 20m away, looking out onto the street in front and from our bedroom at the back affording a view over a vacant meadow under the walls about the size of three football pitches. Here we were delighted to discover that a band of visiting Viking traders had laid out a longboat and were explaining to onlookers how they built it, and from their camp fire offering a taste of Viking

Up the Jerzual. View through Le Petit Port, Margaret in the background

...and down. View from Le Petit Port. (Yes, that's me!)

food to those willing to risk it. A band of troubadours performed just under our window, their playing of medieval instruments occasionally accompanied by a troupe of dancers performing a round and inviting spectators to join in and learn the very simple movements – usually nothing much more complicated than a sideways step-and-a-hop and then in reverse while keeping time with the music.

Dinan-Port

At the bottom of the Jerzual is Dinan-Port, where in the past goods transported by river from the coast were unloaded and lugged up to the town on pack animals or by sweating porters. Nowadays it's a picturesque quarter with a medieval bridge still used (carefully!) by motor vehicles, and with a row of roadside restaurants and cafés along the river bank. There are also several restaurants actually on the Jerzual itself, in one of which on one occasion I received an unexpected bonus. I'd been placing our order in French – despite, or perhaps because, the place was full of loud English tourists barking at the waiting staff in English and I wanted to reassure the proprietor that we aren't all like that. When we'd finished our main course he came over, leaned conspiratorially over my shoulder and whispered, *'Do you know what a 'trou normand' is?'*. *'Yes'*, I replied, *'it's a small glass of Calvados to clear the palate between courses.*' Whereupon he reached into his top pocket and produced two glasses and placed them on the table in front of us and filled them with the said spirit. I took this to be a mark of appreciation for being clients who were polite to him and his staff, and who didn't assume that the louder we shouted at them in English the more likely it would be that they'd understand. Since that memorable occasion ownership of the restaurant has changed – twice – but it's still an atmospheric place to eat and in colder weather there is the added pleasure of watching meat being roasted on its open hearth.

I'm sure other towns in France would challenge this eulogy with counter-claims, and they may well be right – it's just that I haven't found them yet. As you read in the first letter in this book, we have several times been to Harfleur for their *fête*, but it can't begin to compare as it's only a tiny fraction of the size of Dinan, lacks a medieval centre full of half-timbered buildings and its walls have long since disappeared (a few stubby remnants stand a metre or so high down by the river). I actually prefer to be in Dinan when it's not the *Fête*, simply because not being packed with actors and re-enactors and an influx of tourists who've come to watch them it's more likely I'll be able to get a table at a favourite restaurant or créperie without having to book or wait a long time if I haven't.

But had it not been for Claude's generosity all those years ago we would never have found it in the first place, so wouldn't have enjoyed for a couple of decades the recurrent pleasure of a short stay or stopover to renew our familiarity with the Old Town and savour Breton cuisine down beside the river or on the Jerzual.

August 1990

POSTSCRIPT
The most frightening thing in the world is sitting in a restaurant within earshot of two waiters who are looking at you, and overhearing one say to the other, 'Well, he ate it.'

Goodnight.

K

KIMRY

Twinning makes the strain

[Conversations in italics were in Russian]

Most commonly 'town twinning' is an English town twinned with one in France of similar size and with possibly some economic similarity – Eastleigh, where I live, was twinned back in 1963 with Villeneuve-St-Georges on the outskirts of Paris because both were 'railway towns'. As our French twin was also twinned with a town in Württemberg we ended up with a three-way twinning to include Germany. Each year our mayors exchange visits or send a representative to lay wreaths at the commemoration of the Armistice in 1918, which so far as I know is unique.

Kornwestheim, in what was then West Germany, was also twinned with a town in East Germany and through them with a town in the Soviet Union – Kimry, astride the Volga some 70kms or so north-west of Moscow. Being in the 'rich' West, the good burghers of Kornwestheim offered economic help to their twin towns, such as when they refurbished a factory they gave the old equipment to their poorer twin to replace equipment there which was even older and even less efficient.

One of the purposes of twinning is to increase mutual understanding. So when your guests arrive you meet them, take them for a meal, both sides make speeches and present formal gifts and then over the next day or so – twinning visits seldom last more than three days – show them the highlights of your town: a visit to a factory or school, a site of historic interest if you have one, a nice restaurant in a bucolic setting – you get the idea. And a tour of your Town Hall or similar building, where the Mayor or his substitute tries to explain how local government works and you try to work out how it compares with the way you do it in your own country.

The inevitable problem is: what to put in, what to leave out. You can't get it all in in three days. The problem is, we all try. The inevitable result is that the visitors are walked off their feet, get overtired with the strain of listening to protracted explanations in a language they don't understand and which then has to be translated – requiring even more concentration, especially if you're out of doors, trying to hear against a background of traffic or wind. On the assumption that your visitors will only visit your town the once, you are determined to show them *everything*. The truth is, many of those visitors will come again on a subsequent 'twinning' visit. In my own case, for example, I went for the first time when Margaret was Mayor, then nine years later I was Mayor myself so another round of visits – leaving aside other occasions in between as part of a delegation jointly celebrating an anniversary of some kind and finally accompanying Margaret again when she was Mayor for a second time.

The Russians would like us in Eastleigh to make it a four-way twinning, but that isn't likely because of the distance and the consequent travel costs. However, our Twinning Association is a different matter, because we have no public funding and our members are enthusiasts who believe in the cultural value of twinning and we pay our own way out of our own pockets. That was the situation when the mayor of Kimry invited us – the Twinning Association – to send a delegation. We'd pay for our visas and our fares to Moscow, he would host us once we got to Russia.

Corridor in the Sovietsky Historical Hotel

Our first problem was Moscow's traffic, and its customary gridlock meant that we took two hours just to get from the airport to our hotel. Because of our delayed arrival our hosts decided that it was too late to proceed home so put us up instead in the Sovietsky Historical Hotel, built in 1952 on Stalin's orders but in the grandiose style of the mid-nineteenth century. Very sumptuous! Even had a harpist to provide a soothing background during breakfast, who was very appreciative when I sought her out to thank her.

Our hosts thought that we shouldn't come to Moscow and leave straightaway without being given a tour of Red Square and seeing the Kremlin. A splendid idea – but when we duly arrive in Kimry itself what are you going to omit from the programme to allow sufficient time? You see where this is going?

Then yet another delay before departing for our ultimate destination: we were taken to an evening performance of a new rock opera in a wonderful auditorium. This gave me an opportunity to see for myself just how the Russians – young and old and of both sexes – dress up for an occasion. They could certainly teach us in England – especially our young people – a thing or two! One would expect the young and sexy to dress fashionably, but I'd never seen so many high heels on shoes and boots. All ages seemed to have dress sense and natural flair.

Our hosts managed something of a gastronomic *tour de force* by introducing us to the cuisine of Ukraine and Azerbaijan in restaurants in Moscow and then in Kimry laying on a folk group to sing and play for us at a dinner of typical Russian dishes.

On the last night we were taken 20kms out to a yacht club on the Volga, where in summer rich Muscovites come to enjoy the river, though at this time of year – April – ice fishing (making a hole in the ice and sitting over it hoping to catch a fish) was still possible in the shallows (the main river was by now free-flowing). As the dinner progressed so did the jokes (more and more risqué!) and then our principal guide (who didn't speak any English, she just looked after us and made sure no one got left behind when the bus moved on) sang a folk song and invited us to respond. No one volunteered, because she had a very nice voice and we knew none of us was that good. However, in such a situation national pride comes into play. I leaned across and observed to the mayor that we'd been in Russia for four days criss-crossing the Volga and through the window at this very moment there it was shining in the dim moonlight, and so far no one had sung us the Volga Boat Song. He murmured that he wasn't much of a singer, so I said, in Russian, *'Well, if you won't sing it, I shall have to'*, not letting on that I only knew one verse. I went over to our hostess and said, *'Come on, Tatiana, you and me – a duet!'*. I don't think our Russian hosts will forget the role reversal of having an Englishman singing the Volga Boat song to *them*, and it will always be one of my most hilarious memories – and at the same time serendipitous for being sung while actually able to see the eponymous river.

Historically, Kimry was renowned for its shoemaking industry – they were the official suppliers of boots for the Russian army which fought Napoleon, and a boot is featured on the town's coat of arms. The visits to factories, schools, clinics and young people's activity centres left me with a strong impression that despite economic difficulties Kimry seemed to offer far more to its young people than would be the case in an English town of comparable size (50,000 inhabitants). The civic authorities provide the venue and the staff and expect the parents to pay for their children's personal equipment, e.g. their costumes if their hobby is, say, dance. At a time when here in England the government is cutting funding for youth clubs, the contrast is stark. I remember half a century ago sitting in the youth hostel in Bremen and asking the warden who built it, and being told 'Hitler'. Stalin had the same vision when he built his 'Pioneers Palaces': provide young people with somewhere where they all want to go because there's so much to do there, and you keep them off the streets, out of trouble and in many cases allow them to acquire a skill in, say, music, theatre or sport. If young people grow up loving their country because of what it gives them then when the time comes they will defend it – which may have been his intention all along (in a military sense). Our wish might be more peaceful though no less imperative: that our children grow up wanting to defend our country's values of freedom of speech, toleration of differences between people, racial harmony, sexual equality and so on. A sound investment?

I mentioned economic problems. The roads were in general in a poor state in the town, with wide holes which led our driver to weave all over the road to avoid them. Outside my second floor hotel room was a fire escape. At least, there was a door leading to an iron platform, with a stair leading – well, it didn't lead anywhere because the metal staircase was lying on the ground below where it had fallen after rusting through. 'In case of fire, go through the emergency door and, *er* – jump!'

Then there were the wooden houses dotted around the town which we'd assumed were derelict but which were in a poor state of repair simply because the owners couldn't afford to modernise

The fire escape outside my hotel room. On the left of the platform the ladder to the ground has rusted away!

them. We were taken to a home for children rescued from abusive parents where some had run away from their own homes to escape violence and find sanctuary; that other endemic Russian phenomenon, excessive drinking amongst the male population, remains a problem.

I've always enjoyed twinning visits and the opportunity to see more of another country, talk to its inhabitants and learn more about its culture, its current problems and how it's tackling them – whether visiting in my official capacity (when I had one) at public expense, or privately, paying my own way. In my experience the Russians and Germans are more internationally-minded than the English, with the French somewhere in between. People who've gone through the standard English education system seldom have reasonable command of any foreign language, unlike their contemporaries on the continent. Is this cause or effect? I'm not sure.

In the restaurant

Because the programme constantly overran we never had time to go shopping and spend some of our roubles until on the final morning on the way to the airport we stopped off at the Sunday market. An unusual feature were stalls selling brightly coloured paper flowers – something to brighten up the long Russian winter when fresh ones would be too expensive for most ordinary people. Inside the covered market hall the stalls were packed tightly together, and I bought some very tasty biscuits and admired the profusion of fresh fish and meat which we for obvious reasons couldn't buy. I also bought a short-handled brush, exactly what I wanted to sweep the floor of my garden shed. As our luggage was all packed ready to go on the plane I had to just push it under the strap round my case and hope they wouldn't make a fuss at the baggage check-in. When questioned, I explained that it was a last-minute present for my wife – which elicited approving smiles. When I said we didn't have brushes like this in England one of them laughed out loud and remarked to me – in English – that he was glad that Russia was more advanced than England. English-speaking Russian border officials with a sense of humour? What a contrast with the Soviet era when I made my first visit!

April 2011

POSTSCRIPT

The village pub had always had an earth floor sprinkled with sawdust and was only licensed to sell home-brewed beer and scrumpy.

New owners had smartened it up, starting with a proper floor and a spirits licence.

Two old farm labourers were slumped over their beer when one grumbled to his mate, 'Oi loiked this place t' way 't used t' be. Oi don't 'arf miss that spittoon.'

'Yer durned fool,' said his mate. 'Yer always did.'

Goodnight.

L

Tripoli

Benghazi

LIBYA

'I'm from Brum!'

These words spoken to me over half a century ago are still fresh in my mind, and I have never ceased to wonder at the quirks of memory – how one can forget important things, but something of absolutely no apparent consequence can stay firmly fixed in one's mind.

Perhaps it wasn't what was said, but by whom and where. By an Arab teenager, of all people, just outside Tripoli, of all places. This is how it happened.

Having been in Malta for some nine months and nearing the end of my time as a national serviceman, I was due some leave. I couldn't afford to go where most other naval personnel went when they had long leave, namely to Sicily – midshipmen weren't paid much and even though I had just shipped my first ring and was now a Sub-Lieutenant I hadn't held the rank long enough to have accumulated any savings. It looked as though I'd be confined to days out, which wasn't a very attractive prospect as I'd already visited nearly all Malta's historic and pre-historic sites during weekends and odd days off, using the local bus service. There was, of course, the companion island of Gozo. But you can have enough of pre-history and vast churches. Some other time, perhaps. What I want is a change.

As luck would have it, the Commander-in-Chief, Lord Mountbatten, was a friend of King Idris of Libya and decided to pay him a visit. Not on his own or by air; he'd take a cruiser and give the ship's company a bit of sea training to justify the expense. I enquired if they had any spare berths, and was told that there was space in the midshipmen's quarters. As I was officially on leave I wouldn't have to do anything, I could just be a passenger. The thought of a free trip, sitting in the gunroom swigging gin and all the mids calling me 'Sir', appealed. As a bonus, I'd leave Europe for the first time and get in a few days in North Africa in a country I wouldn't otherwise have much chance of getting to.

Anchored off Tripoli, the C-in-C hosted a party for local dignitaries. Attendance by officers was compulsory, including passengers – I might be excused duties, but that didn't extend to exemption from the duty of assisting with hospitality. So I had my first experience of trying to entertain and engage with people with whom I had no common language, our guests being Libyan army and navy officers who spoke only Arabic. Also, of course, being Muslims they didn't drink alcohol, so we couldn't resort to the armed forces' age-old method of breaking the ice with incomprehensible foreigners: ply your guests with copious booze, get 'em plastered and then even if your verbal communication doesn't extend beyond the equivalent of 'Cheers!' at least when they wake up next day in their own beds having been carried ashore paralytic they'll remember that they had a really good time with you last night and will regard you ever after as a friend. What other justification is there for diplomatic receptions, if not that? What better justification does one *need*?

Being, as I said, officially on leave, I was free to spend as much time ashore as I wanted. I managed one serious visit, to the ruins of the famous Roman amphitheatre at Sabratha. Four of us hired a jeep, and while doing so were accosted by some likely lads from the locality who attempted to worm their way into our company for reasons best known to themselves but which you can probably guess at as well as we could at the time. They were after our money, whether by over-charging us for some service or other or, if that didn't work, then straightforward pocket-picking would do. They spoke English with good accents, but it rapidly became evident that they had not learned it at school – they'd probably never been to school – but from the radio. So when one of them asked me where I came from and I said 'Portsmouth', he replied with the phrase at the top of this story: 'I'm from Brum'. I'm sure he didn't know what it meant, it was just something he'd heard someone say on the wireless, and he'd mimicked it. He had no idea that 'Brum' was a very particular place in England, in fact Birmingham, England's second city, and that anyone who came from it would have for starters a distinctive Brummie accent. We needed no further evidence that these were young lads on the make, and we got into our jeep and headed out into the desert as fast as we could before they had a chance to make their next move.

The Roman Theatre of Sabratha.

I was surprised to see just how narrow the cultivated coastal strip was, just a couple of miles inland and agriculture appeared to stop dead and the land dissolved into desert. Nowadays I suppose everyone knows this, everyone's seen the films, documentaries and TV travelogues and read the colour supplements. But back in the early 50s we were not so aware of the outside world. TV was in black-and-white, and so expensive that most households didn't have it anyway. The full-colour travel programmes we are nowadays all familiar with were yet to be made, so all I knew about the Libyan Desert was what I'd read about in books, not seen in pictures. So seeing it at first hand was, in the true sense of the phrase, an 'eye-opener'.

We stayed only a few days in Tripoli before raising anchor and heading for the country's second city, Benghazi, where in the market I bought as a small souvenir a Tripolitanian camel pipe, which to this day hangs on my conservatory wall. I explain to visitors that it is entirely authentic, and is exactly as played by Tripolitanian camels. I recall seeing a banana tree for the first time – again, commonplace nowadays when virtually everyone goes to Spain on holiday and has seen such things from toddlerhood. But this tale is set in the 50s, before foreign holidays in the sun were the norm. For as long as most of us can remember Libya was ruled by Colonel Gadaffi, yet who was it I said the C-in-C was going to see? Yes, the *King*. Few nowadays will remember him, or even know Libya ever even *had* kings.

But I still remember those pushy Arab teenagers who might have fooled us into thinking they were genuinely friendly had one of them not lobbed in those fatally inappropriate and unlikely words in just too perfect English, to whom I would nowadays probably reply, 'My other leg plays '*The Bluebells of Scotland*' '.

July 1954

POSTSCRIPT
There are three types of bison: the North American, the European and the pudding.

Goodnight.

M

MACAU

Sardines!

I'd always wanted to go to Hong Kong, as when I was a small boy Pa – my grandfather – had told me many stories of his time on the Far East Station in the 1890s and I'd seen photos of himself dressed in Chinese costume when he'd gone ashore somewhere up the Yangtze – something apparently lots of sailors did for a souvenir; and two, a pile of heads, all with pigtails, after a spate of executions.

But the place which fascinated me even more was Macau.

Adrian had moved to Hong Kong in 1985 with his wife, Myrtle (my sister-in-law) and their two sons, Paul and Matthew, and spent his time flying around the Pacific capitals on business. But he took time off at Christmas, and had invited Margaret and I to join them for the festive season. He agreed to take us on a day-trip to Macau, mainly because he wanted to take us to Hernando's Hideaway, a noted restaurant which served Portuguese cuisine out on one of the islands away from the town itself. He hired a vehicle something like a glorified golf buggy the moment we landed, and we piled in and headed off over the new bridge which now connected all the islands and had replaced the ferries which for centuries had been the only connection. It seemed strange ordering from a menu in Portuguese proffered by a Chinese waiter, when being about as far from Portugal as it was possible to get. After the meal we drove to the far end of the second island, Coloane, where we were able to visit the chapel dedicated to St Francis Xavier, a Jesuit missionary who in the mid-sixteenth century brought the gospel to the Far East as far as Japan and died on an island near Macau in 1552. There are also relics of priests martyred for their faith.

Chapel of St Francis Xavier

A Portuguese frigate was anchored offshore, flying the ensign aft. Nothing very spectacular about that, you might say. Macau was a Portuguese possession, so why shouldn't they have a warship there and of course it would be flying the national flag. But it was by the time of our visit the *last remaining* Portuguese possession, the last surviving remnant of the Portuguese overseas empire which had collapsed in the 1970s and it only remained in Portuguese hands because the Chinese refused to accept it back so long as Hong Kong remained British. The other thought which came into my mind was how small an area Macau occupied, and I tried to picture a wartime map of the Far East when everywhere for a thousand miles or more in any direction was under Japanese occupation and coloured black and right in the middle was this tiny, *tiny* pin-prick of white – neutral, because neither Japan nor Portugal had declared war on the other. It must have been a strange experience for the inhabitants at that time, completely surrounded as they were by the armies of a country which was massacring Chinese everywhere else but which stopped its troops at their border out of diplomatic niceties because the Chinese there were Portuguese subjects and even though the colony was theirs for the taking had they been so minded.

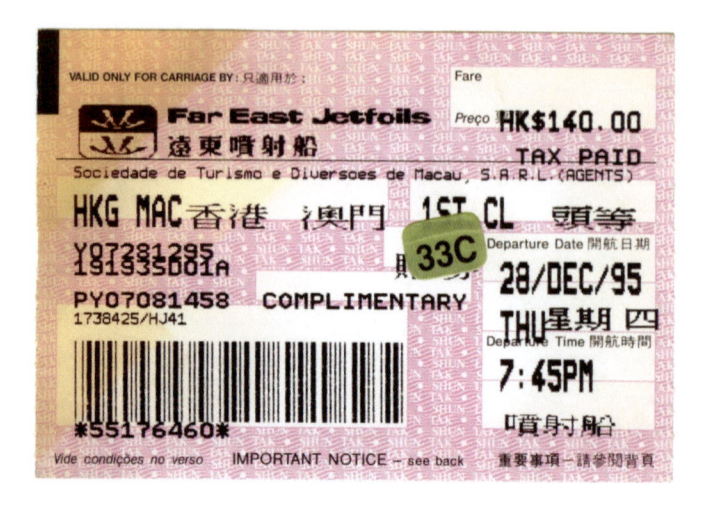

The second time we visited, five years later, we were on our own. Well, on our own insofar as we were the only Europeans; the boat was absolutely packed with Hong Kong Chinese all set for a day out, mostly to the casinos. Gambling was banned in China, and even in Hong Kong the only betting permitted was at the races. If you wanted to chance your luck at the tables, you had to take the ferry to Macau. Which many did at weekends.

But we were in for a rough crossing. A storm was brewing, and as the boat hit the first large wave and bounced all the Chinese passengers shrieked with glee. Another wave, a bit stronger. More whoops.

'This is going to end in tears.'

'But *we're British*. Mustn't let the old country down, stiff upper lip and all that. Think of the Empah, what? Show the natives what it was that made the British Empah great.'

So we sat tight, clenched our stomachs and swallowed hard. For an hour, at least. Being sea-sick when we were the only Europeans on board would have been just too hideously embarrassing. We managed to hold out, but it was not an experience I would want to repeat. I am, after all, decidedly *not* a good sailor even though I got in a fair bit of sea time when I was in the Navy, and I don't like it when it's rough.

By the time we reached Macau all the other passengers were decidedly the worse for wear, a lot had been visibly ill and the rush to get on to dry land would have finished off anyone with a weak heart. Every man for himself, and as for the women – they used their elbows. Once on shore we were hit by driving rain, and the wind was so strong it blew my umbrella inside out. What were we supposed to do? We'd come to potter round the town, but we'd get soaked if we did.

When in a strange town and it's pissing down there is one reliable stratagem. Lunch. At least we'd be in the dry.

Sardines seemed a strange dish to order, as a staple of Portugal but on the wrong side of the world, washed down with *Mateus Rosé* in that distinctive-shaped bottle. But when in Rome, etc. Despite being entirely surrounded by oriental faces we were not in China,

The Senate Square

but in a part of metropolitan Portugal. Macau was quintessentially, aggressively, perhaps even desperately, Portuguese, had been for four centuries even if only on a microscopic scale and it was going to stay that way until the day it was handed back to the government in Beijing regardless of the fact that the date for this occurrence had actually been set and everyone knew there were barely a couple of years left before the Macanese took their orders from there instead of from Lisbon. At the end of 1997 the sun would finally set on the Portuguese Empire of overseas possessions, other than Madeira and the Azores where the inhabitants really are Portuguese and predominantly European. All-ee same-ee Goa, and after the War the French didn't quibble or stand on ceremony in handing over Pondicherry when India became independent.

We'd set out intending to spend a day wandering about the main and back streets of this time-capsule mini-state, but in such weather it was best to accept an unkind fate and abort – there was just no point in hanging about. Best see if we can get an earlier boat back. Such a good idea that almost everyone else who'd been on

The façade of the former cathedral.

the boat with us that morning had had it too – the terminus was absolutely jam-packed and it was almost impossible to move, let alone get to the ticket kiosk and enquire. Margaret was given the brush-off twice by a ticket clerk, when fortunately a Chinese in a tweed jacket, smoking a pipe and looking every inch the country gent reminded us in perfect English that this was the Orient and not the West and manners were different. Turned out he'd been a diplomat in Vienna, and was aware of the contrast between how officials treat the public in the West and in the East. He helped us get our bookings changed. So we did strike lucky and get an earlier boat back, repeating our earlier demeanour of stiff British upper lip and air of 'You call this rough weather? Why, back home we get worse than this on village duck ponds.'

December 1995

POSTSCRIPT
You can never be sure with a bishop. It's always a case of mitre might not.

Goodnight.

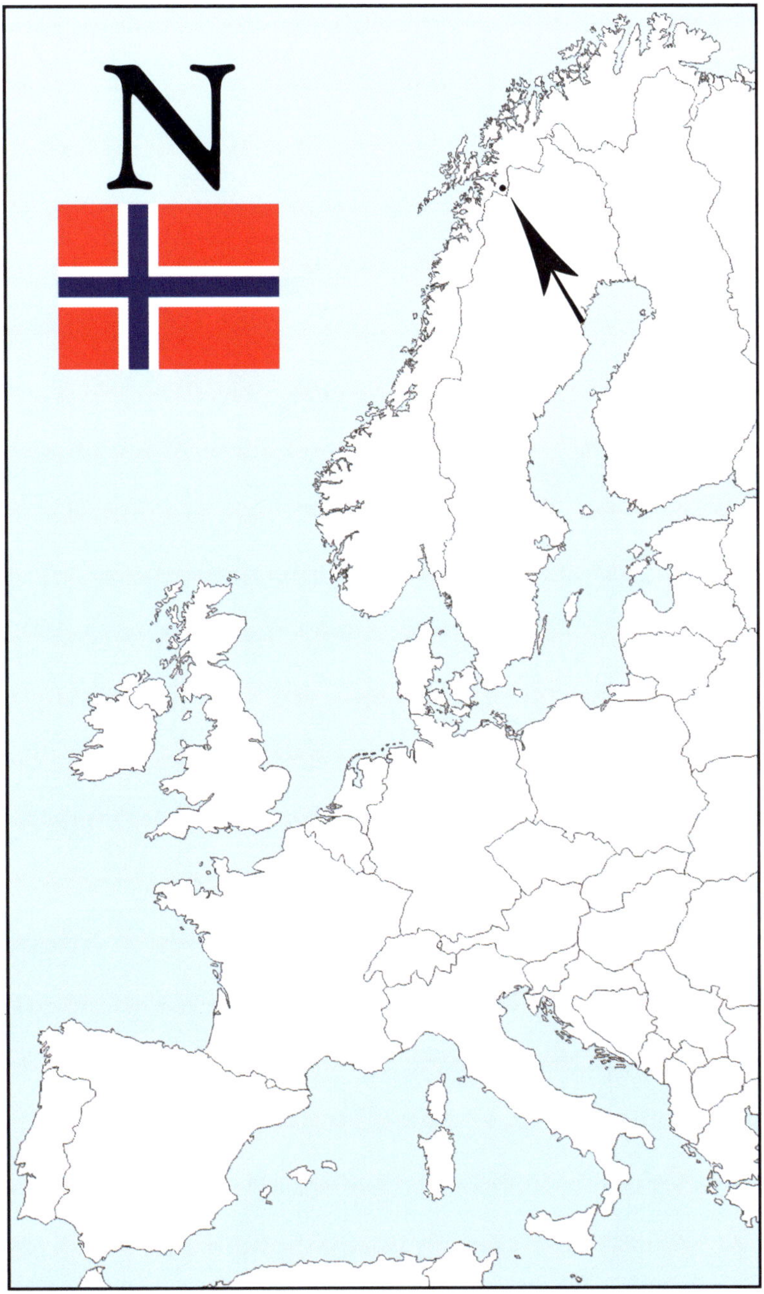
N

NARVIK

Phew!

It had taken us a whole day to get from Brekkvasselv to Majavatn, and we still needed – somehow – to get to Narvik and a lift was the only direct way. 'If we can't get a lift, what's Plan B?'
'Get the train.'
'There's no railway from here to Narvik.'
'No. The train goes across the border into Sweden, where we can change and get a train north to Kiruna. The Swedes have to have a railway up there because it's an iron mining area. Swedish ports on the Gulf of Bothnia are frozen up in the winter, so they export it via Narvik because it's an ice-free port.'

We set off for the station – well, halt – and found that there was a train at one o'clock – and that was the only one. They had just one a day. So – we've got till one o'clock to get a lift, and if no luck then after a day and a half of standing here we give up and proceed on public transport. Hope we can find the money.

Ten o'clock came, no luck. Eleven. Nossink. Twelve. Nowt. Give up, better get down to the station – sorry, halt – in case it's early. Hang on – there's a car coming – one last try. Bugger me – it stopped!

The driver and his friend had just been down to Trondheim to buy a car, had found what they wanted and were off to sign on in the Norwegian Air Force for their national service. And where would this be? Bugger me again – Tromsø, some way beyond Narvik. That's over five hundred kilometres north of here! Now that's what I *call* a lift!

We put our gear in the boot, and settled into the back seats. Having no common language, conversation was virtually impossible. Signs. We'll stop here for lunch, you pay for yours, we'll pay for ours. Stop for coffee, we insisted on paying. Here we are at the spot where the road crosses the Arctic Circle, so let's stop and look at the monument and do what all tourists do: pose standing astride the line across the road with one foot in the Arctic and

one not. Keep going, but there's no continuous road to Narvik. It stops at the shore of the fjord and you take the car ferry across to the shore opposite, likely as not just a small uninhabited islet, drive across it to get the next ferry and then continue in this disjointed manner and we have to make it to the first of the ferries at Fauske before they shut down the service for the night. We didn't make it. As we drove down to the shingle, there was the little ferry heading out into the sound.

What now?

We'll just have to stop here for the night, and catch the first ferry when they start again in the morning. We couldn't all sleep inside the vehicle, so by signs we indicated that we'd leave it to them and we'd sleep outside. Seemed only fair, and anyway we had groundsheets and sleeping bags, which they hadn't.

I got out first and did a quick reccy. There were no buildings, not even a ticket office or whatever, to provide any shelter – though luckily it was fine, dry and midsummer – midnight sun, and all that; the road ran through a totally empty landscape and stopped at the water's edge where the ferry came up to the shingle; passengers just got on the ferry if it was there, or hung around if it wasn't until it came back. The land was strewn with boulders and I searched out one by the roadside with a flat surface as my resting place for the night and went back to the car to retrieve my rucksack and sleeping bag.

As I approached the car I became aware of a strange smell – something like a combination of industrial-strength garlic and the inside of a Japanese wrestler's jockstrap. Getting nearer, it became overpowering. Then I saw that Mike was still in the back of the car, but his face contorted in what looked like the final stages of asphyxiation as he scrabbled dementedly at the door handle in his frantic efforts to get out. He did. He gasped fresh air and his face colour subsided from boiled beetroot to its normal pallor.

'What's up?'

'Can't you smell it?'

'Yes. What is it?'

'The driver took his shoes off!'

When you consider that I could smell it twenty feet away, what must it have been like inside the car? To this day I can't conceive how those two fellers managed to sleep together all night inside the car in such a stench.

The ferry at Fauske was the longest of the several crossings on the road north. At each stop, Mike would leap out of the car and yank off his socks and sandals and plunge his feet into the nearest stream – regardless of the temperature of the water and notwithstanding our experiences at Trondheim with immersion in seawater at such latitudes – to try to get some relief from the mozzies' attentions of the previous night when we'd camped by the lake at Majavatn *(as related in another book in this series – but which one would be telling!)*. We could only guess what the locals thought: 'The English are renowned for their strange customs' – *shrug*. Fortunately, in this part of Norway there was always a stream handy – or the seashore by the ferry landing stage.

Next morning we ate a little chocolate for breakfast, got back in the car, caught the first ferry and arrived without further mishap in Narvik. Hand-shakes all round, thanks very much, good luck. It was midday. We were 200kms north of the Arctic Circle, yet the sun was so fierce we had to stand in the shade to get out of it to look at our town map to locate the youth hostel where we planned to spend the night. As usual, bugger's luck – it was right at the far end of town and up a hill, presumably because it was purpose-built and they'd had to find a suitable piece of land, and beyond the confines of the existing town at the top of a long incline was the only place where they could find a site big enough and cheap enough for their purposes. The view was dominated by a large mound of iron ore brought in by rail from the mines at Kiruna, across the border in

Narvik in the 1950s

Sweden, so no wonder the site was cheap!

I spent a summer in Malta as part of my national service, yet that day in Narvik has stayed in my memory as the hottest day I ever experienced. It sounds unbelievable that North Norway could be hotter than the middle of the Mediterranean – but that's how it felt at the time and how I remember it. So hot that for the first and only time in my hitch-hiking days I stopped dead, sat myself down in some shade and refused to go any further. 'I'm not moving from here until it gets cooler. The hostel won't be open at this time of day anyway.' When at last the hostel opened and I got a bed I more or less collapsed and slept the clock round, so probably I was suffering from mild heatstroke, brought on by the combination of heat and wearing clothing which was too heavy.

Final proof that the temperature wasn't a figment of my imagination came when we saw a cat sitting on a doorstep. You know what? It was so hot he'd got his top button undone.

August 1959

POSTSCRIPT
First housewife: 'I heard that you've recently lost your husband.'
Second housewife: 'Yes.'
First housewife: 'What happened?'
Second housewife: 'He went up the garden to pick a fresh cabbage for Sunday lunch and on the way back down the garden he dropped dead.'
Second housewife: 'That's terrible. What did you do?'
First housewife: 'We opened a tin of peas.'

Goodnight.

O

ÓRZOLA

Corks!

It took me ten years, but I finally made it to La Graciosa, the smallest of the Canary Islands with a resident population (of 700). There are buses to the ferry terminal at Órzola, a small fishing village at the northern tip of Lanzarote noted for its seafood restaurants, but from my time-share in Puerto del Carmen I could never work out a way to get there, catch the ferry and then get back the same day. The situation resolved itself when Mike joined me for a week and said he'd be quite happy to hire a car, as he drives an automatic at home.

Foreign tourists seldom make the crossing to set foot on La Graciosa, but many thousands see it from the Mirador del Rio, a vantage point directly opposite the main settlement, Caleta del Sebo, where the passenger ferry docks. From near the top of the cliffs which dominate the north shore of Lanzarote the viewer enjoys a panoramic view of the whole island from a height of 1,630 feet (nearly 500m). End-to-end it's about eight kilometres by four and, except where a hill gets in the way, you can see it all laid out in front of you. Not that there's much to see. It's rocky, barren and flat, with a few conical hills which rise steeply from the bare terrain as if plonked down from above by some giant chess player, and the dominant colour is brown: rock and sand. There are no trees, nor in fact any signs of anything green, and as there is no natural water source fresh water has to be piped in from Lanzarote. A network of tracks can be seen leading out of Caleta and disappearing into the distance on their way to remote beaches or to the only other cluster of houses, a shoreline hamlet away to the east. A number of pleasure boats can be seen tied up in Caleta's tiny harbour. As one would expect, there are several waterfront cafés ready to greet visitors alighting from the ferry, but all the buildings are one or two storey and from this lofty viewpoint there doesn't appear to be a main square, a church or any large administrative building to act as a focal point.

The previous day we'd picked up the car and I'd taken Mike, nowadays a keen photographer who works with a tripod, to the former capital of Lanzarote, Teguise, because it has a number of eighteenth century houses and some typical Canarian wooden balconies which I thought he would find worth pointing a lens at. There isn't much of historical interest anywhere on the island because in the past it never had a very large population nor many nobles or important officials living in style in grand houses. The reason for this was that until Napoleonic times it was constantly exposed to random raids by Barbary pirates from Morocco, Algiers, Tunis and Tripoli. At that time North Africa was still nominally part of the Ottoman Empire, and the Sultan of Turkey authorised locally-based corsairs to roam the Mediterranean and the Atlantic as privateers and prey on the merchant shipping of Christian countries or raid their coastal villages in return for a share of the profits. In addition to robbery and general pillage these pirates carried captives off to be sold in their slave markets. This ever-present danger inhibited the settlement and development of the Canary Islands, especially of the two closest to Africa, Lanzarote and Fuerteventura.

At the end of the eighteenth century the newly-independent United States faced demands for tribute from the rulers of the Barbary States amounting to almost one-sixth of the entire national budget, and Congress was forced to make a choice: either keep American merchant vessels safe from attack by corsairs by paying regular tribute to the Dey of Algiers, the Pasha of Tripoli *et al*, or build a navy and deal with them once and for all. The Americans' success in the Second Barbary War in 1815 forced the Dey to agree to give up attacking U.S. merchant ships and holding captives for ransom and to return all captives currently held in slavery. The U.S. benefited from knowing that henceforth its merchant vessels would be able to go about their business in safety, but the suppression of piracy was equally beneficial to the inhabitants of all coastal villages and islands in the Atlantic such as the Canaries who hitherto had had to live in constant fear of pirate attacks.

As well as La Graciosa I also wanted to visit the Castillo de Santa Barbara at Teguise, which from the crest of a 450m bluff commands views over much of the centre of the island and out to sea on three sides and houses a museum of piracy. The problem for the tourist is access: it's up a steep, winding dedicated road and there is no bus. Now we have a car, so at last I'll be able to get there. But my stomach tells me it's time for lunch, and on the advice of the charming lady in the tourist office in Teguise we head for her recommended restaurant. Everything nicely timed, and then we'll be off to the castle. Only we hadn't realised that at four o'clock they close the road by lowering a barrier, and when we turned up at twenty past three it was already in place. Aaaaargh! Come back tomorrow.

Tomorrow is planned the trip to La Graciosa, but as we missed out on the *castillo* due to the road being closed we'd better do that on the way, because there won't be another chance – it's Wednesday, Mike's last day before flying home, so now or never. No barrier across the road this time, so on up the switchback access road, wonderful panoramic views over the centre of the island and then park outside the castle. This is impressively inaccessible – a flight of stone steps leads up to a small platform onto which, in former times, a drawbridge would have been lowered at right-angles, and then in through the narrow castle gateway. The guardrooms are now laid out with the story of Spain's attempts to settle the

The only way into the Castillo de Santa Barbara
(and no, you don't have to get past the watchman!)

Canary Islands and the problems with pirates, especially during the seventeenth and eighteenth centuries, and enemy attack during wars with England or France. Everyone knows that Lord Nelson lost his right arm; it's not so well known where he suffered the injury. Answer: during a British attack on Tenerife in 1797.

    The ferry across El Rio, the strait separating Lanzarote from La Graciosa, leaves every hour or so from Órzola and takes a little over half an hour. It's quite a small boat, and we progress gracefully out of the harbour into the strait and the moment we pass the end of the breakwater – BOOM! We're hit by an absolutely enormous swell and bounce about all over the place like a cork in a tumble drier, and first-time passengers could be forgiven for thinking that at any moment we're going to turn turtle and sink with all hands! I'm on the upper deck and hanging on for dear life, but thoroughly enjoying the exhilarating experience because I can see the captain in the wheelhouse and from the expression on his face he is obviously totally unperturbed, so this rolling and pitching must be normal. The harbour of Órzola is protected on the west by the Punta Fariones, a rocky peninsula jutting out into the sea, with a navigation beacon on its point. Once we pass this the open strait is flat calm and the excessive motion stops as suddenly as it started, and we proceed close inshore under the shadow of the cliffs, trying to pick out the Mirador del Rio where we'd been the previous day. We make landfall in the harbour of Caleta without further excitement.

I can quite see why holidaymakers enthuse about going to La Graciosa with their children for a day out on the beach – there's sand everywhere, including the streets (instead of tarmac). After a restorative coffee at a café overlooking the harbour and time spent gazing in awe at the lowering cliffs of Lanzarote on the other side of El Rio we set off to explore. It doesn't take long. There are only a few dozen houses, several bars, a couple of small shops and supermarkets but, as I'd previously observed from the Mirador, there isn't any sort of built-up town centre with a town hall and also – which surprises me – no signs of a church. A hundred metres or so inland from the harbour the houses come to a dead stop and to our amazement the unmade, sandy track running along behind the last houses is furnished with a row of new lamp posts! What on earth *for* when there isn't any traffic? Where did the money come from, and was the expense justified? A rough track leads away into the distance across a barren landscape, giving access by taxi (visitors can't bring cars) to various remote and deserted beaches.

A question I often ask myself when visiting out-of-the-way places: what do the people who live here permanently do with themselves in their leisure time? Tourists don't mind the lack of things to do – they've come to relax or perhaps, as is certainly the case here, admire the view or enjoy the quiet beach and watch the children splashing about in the shallow water. But if you *live* here – what then? You can't spend every leisure hour paddling. No matter how impressive the cliffs of Lanzarote are, you can get fed up with just looking at them and surely you must get frustrated with living in a tiny community when no matter how bored you are there's nowhere else to go? And what if it rains? Villages whose only attraction is a beach are no fun in bad weather!

I'm left with just three of the Canary Islands yet to visit now that I've managed to tick the *'been there'* box with regard to La Graciosa. I shan't be back, but if I had a family of small children I well might.

February 2012

POSTSCRIPT
People often think that Morris dancing is easy. On the contrary, it's very complicated.
There are more things in Morris dancing than you can shake a stick at.

Goodnight.

P

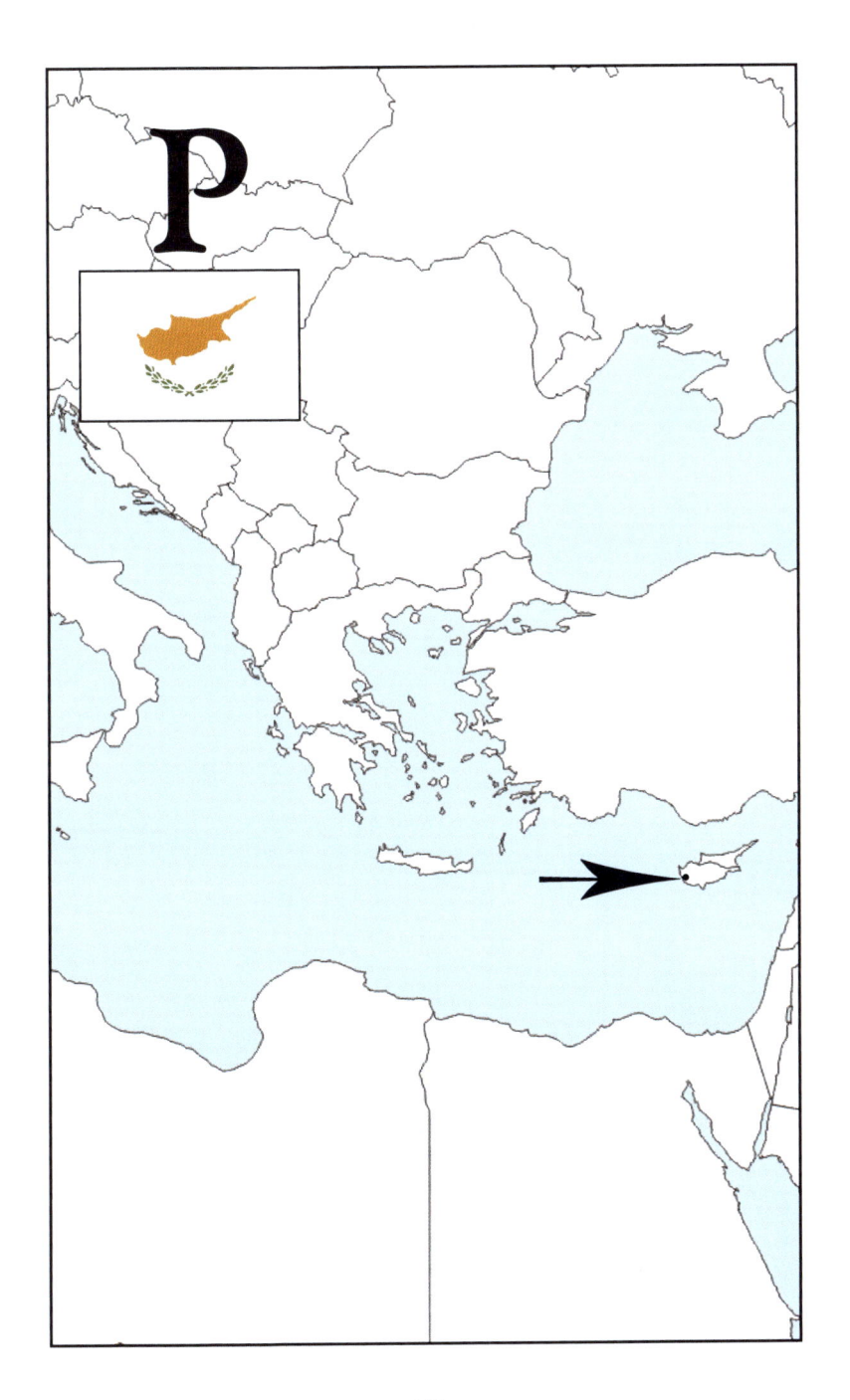

PAPHOS

A tour de force?

I suppose one can say that reaching the age of three-quarters of a century is a significant milestone in life. That's how Margaret and I saw it when I reached that particular watershed, and an invitation to spend the occasion with my brother (Adrian) and sister-in-law (Myrtle) at their house in Cyprus was most welcome. They'd retired there a dozen years before, and built their own house outside Paphos on the west coast of the island to their own design and on the side of a hill, with a commanding view across twenty miles of countryside and no possibility of anyone ever obstructing it – short of building a skyscraper right in front of them (hardly likely). The other attraction was that as my birthday occurs in the middle of March the temperatures in Cyprus are most agreeable, as well as being a welcome alternative to those usual in England at that time of year.

The climate is one of the reasons so many other Brits have done what Adrian and Myrtle decided to do a decade ago: retire to Cyprus – though in their case not from their home in the UK but from Hong Kong. Another is that English is widely spoken or at least understood, the legacy of the island being a British protectorate between 1878 and 1960 and the language of administration being, naturally, that of the colonial power. The problem with the ex-pat community, so far as I could fathom it in a short stay, was that few of them had bothered to learn the local language – the same problem as occurs in those parts of France and Spain which have seen English retirees descend in droves and then set about creating England-over-the-Water rather than integrating with the indigenous population and adopting or adapting to the indigenous language. Granted, Greek may be harder for an English person to learn than French or Spanish – particularly as they almost certainly won't have learnt a bit in school (if they can remember that far back). But surely if you *choose* to go and live somewhere where the local language is Greek, then . . .

There's lot of history in Cyprus! We tend to think of it simply as part of Ancient Greece, but in fact it was settled two millennia BC by people from Asia Minor and remains of those settlements and civilisations are much in evidence in the west of the island. Adrian set about with some enthusiasm showing me each and every mosaic within earshot, then every Mycenaean tomb, then Neolithic remains, Aphrodite's alleged birthplace and the spring named after her ('Aphrodite's Well') and finally the excavated site of Kourion. After a day of being shown archaeological sites followed by another day of another lot and then another, images become blurred and you forget which millenium you're in let alone which day of the week it is. 'Mosaiced out' probably describes my mental state after a week.

To be perfectly honest, much as I enjoy watching archaeological digs on TV I'd never dream of going near one in person, and I have never felt enthused when looking at piles of stones and being told that they were once a round-house or the foundations of a temple or whatever. I'm extremely interested in history but pre-

Tomb of the Kings, Paphos

history leaves me cold. I want names, dates and events. Hadrian's Wall is interesting to me because I can see it and stand on it (and I have), and rather than have to use my imagination I prefer to visit a reconstruction or recreation to get an idea of what it was like to live then and in those conditions.

Getting Cyprus's history into focus is not easy, but if it's OK with you I'll try (if not, skip the next couple of paras). We all have ideas about Ancient Greece and Ancient Rome, even if only from blockbuster movies; most of us learned about them in history lessons in school, some of us even did Latin (me, for one). We then get a bit hazy. We've probably heard of the Byzantine Empire, but that's about it – we've heard of it. No idea where it was, still less when it was and nothing at all about who ruled it. Well, when the western half of the Roman Empire (capital: Rome) finally capitulated to the barbarians in 476 the eastern half (capital: Constantinople) carried on for another thousand years, though it was and remained Greek in character, culture and language and the form of Christianity differed – (Greek) Orthodox as opposed to (Roman) Catholic.

Such trade as there was between Western Europe and the Eastern Mediterranean was conducted by intermediaries – Venetian and Genoese merchants – and direct contact not resumed until the coming of the Crusades seven hundred years later at the end of the eleventh century. The only exceptions were pilgrims, who throughout this time continued to travel to the Holy Land, risking their lives in the process and taking several years to make a round trip (if they ever came back at all, of course, as many perished along the way).

The Venetian castle guarding the harbour at Paphos

In 1191 Richard the Lion Heart was on his way to join the Third Crusade when his fiancée and sister were shipwrecked on Cyprus and the local king, Isaac Comnenus, was a bit flaky in his treatment of his royal visitors/hostages. He made a big mistake in falling out with King Richard, and paid for it by having his kingdom conquered – ending up imprisoned in silver chains (Richard had promised not to put him in irons – so he kept his word, sort of) and dying a couple of years later. Richard was now in possession of Cyprus but didn't know what to do with it, so sold it to the Knights Templar, who the following year sold it on to the titular King of Jerusalem, Guy de Lusignan, whose family remained in possession as kings of Cyprus for the next three hundred years until displaced by the Venetians, who held sway for the next hundred. Thus throughout the entire medieval period Cyprus was an outpost of Western Europe with Catholic kings and the feudal system exploiting the indigenous Greek Orthodox population while surrounded on three sides (look at the map) by lands ruled by Muslims – Palestine, Egypt and Asia Minor. Such an anomaly had a built-in sell-by date, which turned out to be 1571 when the Turks expelled the Venetians. This consolidated Ottoman total control of the Eastern Mediterranean and freed the Turks to embark on a long campaign of conquest in Europe which remained a very real threat right up to the Siege of Vienna in 1689. For the poor old Greek Cypriots and their Orthodox Church it just meant a change of master: feudal lords who were Roman Catholics replaced by Muslim pashas – and for the next three hundred years!

Lunch beside the harbour with my brother and sister-in-law, Adrian and Myrtle (Jessop)

All of which helps to explain why Cyprus has so many medieval castles, of which one of the finest examples is at the harbour mouth in Paphos itself. It's open to the public, and the cells display the casual cruelty of the times when it was in use. But for a modern visitor it provides splendid views across the town and along the coast northwards, so it's well worth walking past the string of restaurants lining the harbour in order to reach it. With fierce competition,

Entrance to the monastery at Kykkos

6th century church at Ayios Georgios

Museum at Ayios Georgios of the Mycenean civilisation which flourished c1300BC

these restaurants provide excellent value and I very much enjoyed a fish *meze* at a table under a most welcome awning alongside tourist boats and touts seeking customers for mini-cruises.

KYKKOS MONASTERY

One of the first religious sites we visited was Ayios Neofytos, a hermitage not far from Paphos, whose principal attraction is a vividly decorated cave where the hermit lived in the twelfth century and which is now accessed by a rickety stairway up the side of the mountain (not recommended if you suffer from vertigo!). Even more sumptuously decorated is the monastery at Kykkos, once almost inaccessible high up in the Troodos Mountains but now easily reached by car thanks to a new road built with EU development funds. The preponderance of gold inside the church reminded me of the cathedral in Seville, with every surface glistening in the light of innumerable candles. But whereas Seville Cathedral has a high ceiling to its nave and so an airy space in which to stand to admire the ornamentation, here in Kykkos the effect is claustrophobic because there is so much of it in a confined space. Moreover, one must observe silence (or at the most, communicate in whispers and risk a sharp disapproving look from one of the ever-present monks). A short walk away is the usual cluster of souvenir stalls selling tourist tat, and also a rather attractive restaurant which at the height of the season must be absolutely packed but which we had almost to ourselves.

One of the finest sites for those interested in the Classical period are the remains of the major trading city of Kourion, just off the main road from Paphos to Limassol. This was founded in the second century BC but fine mosaics recently discovered date from the 5th century AD – and are protected by a huge over-arching roof structure supported on pillars allowing free movement of air. There are remains, too, of an early Christian basilica. The amphitheatre has been fully excavated and even brought back into use – as a venue for concerts. I didn't have an opportunity to experience one, but I can imagine an evening there must be a bit like attending the Minack Theatre near Land's End in Cornwall with the players performing against a backdrop of the open sea – only with the mercury a bit farther up the thermometer!

The north-west corner of Cyprus is a nature reserve, accessible only on foot. But the approach roads are interesting and lead to several favoured spots with beach-side or harbour-side restaurants. The most attractive spot in my opinion is Pomos farther along the north coast towards the Turkish Cypriot enclave of Kokkina. I was not overly impressed by the food on offer ('ordinary' would perhaps be a fitting description!) but from our table the relaxing view across the little harbour with its complement of small fishing boats and pleasure craft tied up alongside the jetty was adequate compensation.

March 2008

POSTSCRIPT
Notice alongside the washbasins in a public toilet:
After using this towel you are advised to wash your hands.

Goodnight.

Q

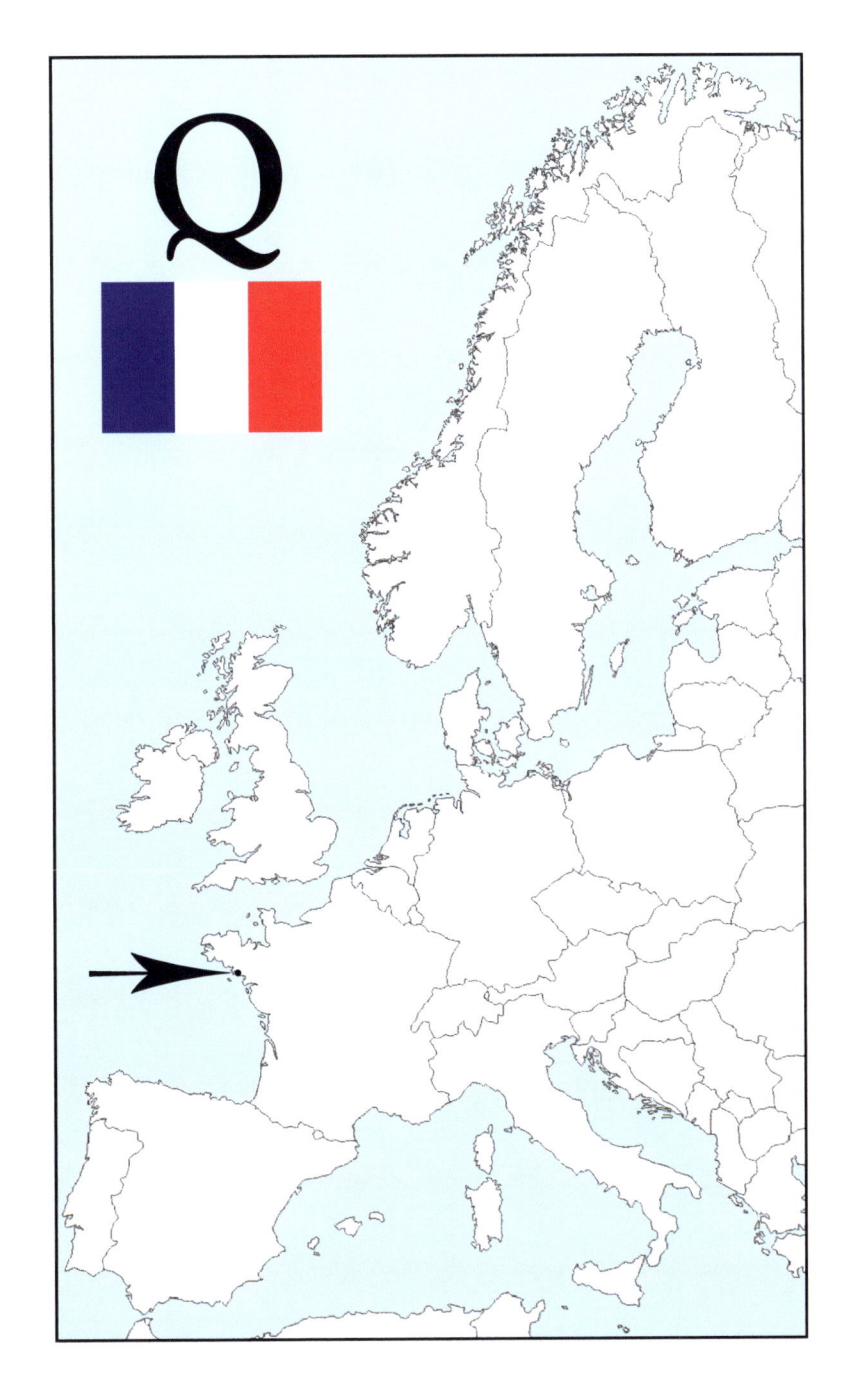

QUIBERON

Belle Île or bust!

I was over seventy before I finally made it to Quiberon, which I first heard of at school when we learned about the Seven Years' War with France which at least so far as naval warfare was concerned served as a dress rehearsal for the Napoleonic Wars forty years later. The Battle of Quiberon Bay in November 1759 was one of Britain's most decisive naval victories. It had the knock-on effect of making it impossible for the French fleet to send reinforcements to their colonists fighting in Canada, with the result that French Canada fell to the British and that country's future as a British possession was secured.

Quiberon is an attractive town, and I hope one day to stay for a proper visit. The journey there by car is fun, as it's at the end of a very long peninsula connected to the mainland by an isthmus only a couple of hundred metres wide, so of course there's only one way on or off – made even narrower because the road has to share the width with a railway line which carries tourists in the summer. But once on the *presqu'île* ('half-island' – interestingly, the Russians use a similar term to designate such geographical features), it's wide enough at some points to have side roads and smaller settlements with clusters of local shops and it's possible to drive along some of the coast away from the main spine road. Once you reach the far end and the waterfront, there are ferries to the three islands off the coast: Belle Île, the largest of the French Atlantic islands, and also Houat and Hoedic, which mean 'duck' and 'duckling' in Breton and lie farther out. These two have tiny permanent populations, and although they cater for visitors in season there's not much to do. *(Sounds ideal!)*

Belle Île, on the other hand, is not so much 'popular' as 'overrun'. When we got there we were told by our guide that they have 5,000 permanent residents but 100,000 tourists a year. The result is that in high summer the cafés and restaurants can't cope, so unless you've booked a table you'll be lucky to find anywhere to eat.

The purpose of our visit was not to explore Quiberon but simply to use it as a jumping-off point for Belle Île. Easier said than done. OK, there are frequent ferries. But there are also kiosks vying with each other to sell visitors a coach tour on arrival – which seemed to us a good idea and a lot cheaper than taking the car, especially as we were only going for the day. But although with the benefit of hindsight a ticket from a kiosk for a coach trip on Belle Île doesn't as a matter of course also include the cost of the ferry to get there, they don't actually make a point of telling you that. It's not unreasonable to think that having bought your ticket, it's 'all inclusive'. But it wasn't, as we found out the minute we tried to proceed to board and were firmly directed to the queue at the ticket kiosk. With only fifteen minutes to departure, we had a fine old time worrying as the chap at the front of the queue seemed to be buying returns, season tickets and half price for children for his own extended family and several others besides, using up his OAP coupons and offering to pay by cheque drawn on the Royal Bank of Uzbekistan. Everyone was muttering and shifting from one foot to the other as he and the cashier argued and as fast as she showed him one set of papers he asked for another set and so it went on and on. We did manage to get a ticket in time, but only just.

That queue was my second major panic. The first was parking to go and see if I could get a ferry ticket anyway – i.e. it's July, the height of the season, was there room? – and having ascertained that there was I then discovered that there was no designated car park for ferry passengers. Where do you find an all-day car park in a major tourist town unaided and at short notice? Answer: you don't. I just went to the first one I could find with a vacant space, parked and left a hastily-scribbled note on my dashboard on the back of a till receipt, grovelling to the parking attendant that I couldn't find anywhere else and was going to Belle Île for the day and would he be kind enough to overlook the fact that I was in a car park with a time limit. I just had to hope that he would take pity on a foreigner and not impose a fine, and while taking in the sights of Belle Île I'd be able to worry about what would be pinned to my windscreen wipers when we got back or even whether the car would still be there, having been towed away and impounded.

> EXCUSEZ-MOI, S'IL
> VOUS PLAÎT.
> HORODATEUR NE MARCHE
> PAS ET JE VAIS SUR LE
> BATEAU À BELLE-ÎLE!!

From Quiberon on a clear day you can just about make out Houat, but Belle Île is clearly visible as it's only 14km away. The crossing to the main town on the island, Le Palais, takes 45 minutes, and once there we found our way to the coach park and were taken for a twenty minute ride as far as Sauzon, the island's second town, for a coffee break and a chance to have a look round.

Waterfront at Sauzon.

From April to September there is a direct ferry from Quiberon and in July and August also from Lorient (foot passengers only). Once back on the bus, our destination was the northern tip of the island to be shown the fort bought in 1894 by the famous French actress Sarah Bernhardt (1844-1923) and the private houses she built nearby for her family and friends. She's hardly a name to conjure with nowadays, but in her day she was probably the most famous actress in the world – and she also played in some early silent films. On an islet just off the north-west coast is the Pointe des Poulains lighthouse, accessible on foot at low tide.

Even on a fairly calm summer's day the Atlantic rollers were crashing onto the cliffs, and one can easily imagine how dramatic it must be in the winter during a gale. It's hardly surprising that the entire western side of Belle Île, facing the open ocean, is a succession of wild indented cliffs and is known as *'le côte sauvage'*. In complete contrast the eastern – sheltered – side of the island has gentle sandy beaches.

Back in Le Palais, we admired the fort built by the Louis XIV's military architect Vauban, famous for his defensive structures to be found all over France – principally on the coast to keep out the filthy British. Of these, the *Ville Close* at Concarneau is to my mind the most remarkable, as the fortifications enclose an urban village which although generally thronged with tourists is still a wonderful day out for a visitor because of all the shops and restaurants.

We didn't have time to visit the fort, as by now it was time to find some lunch. Not as easy as you might think. The influx of visitors means that during the summer the population rises to 25,000 and at the very peak in late July-early August to a staggering 35,000. It was hardly surprising that in high season none of the restaurants overlooking the fort or the harbour had an empty table and we only managed to find a place which could feed us by going up a side street to try our luck.

Back in Quiberon we found the car just as I'd left it. Either the attendant had humoured a visitor, or no one had come to check. I like to think it was an example of French *'sympathie'*, but I'll never know. Time now to find a seafood restaurant and enjoy *fruits de mer* – it's what you do in coastal towns in Brittany. No? Well, it's what *we* do, given half a chance. Quiberon's commercial fishing harbour lies on the eastern side of the peninsula protected from the open ocean, but the ferries operate on the south side, facing the Atlantic, and this is where the main tourist shops, cafés and restaurants lie. Unlike on Belle Île, we were spoilt for choice!

July 2007

POSTSCRIPT
As the man said: 'Just because I look like a fool it doesn't mean to say that I'm not!'

Goodnight.

R

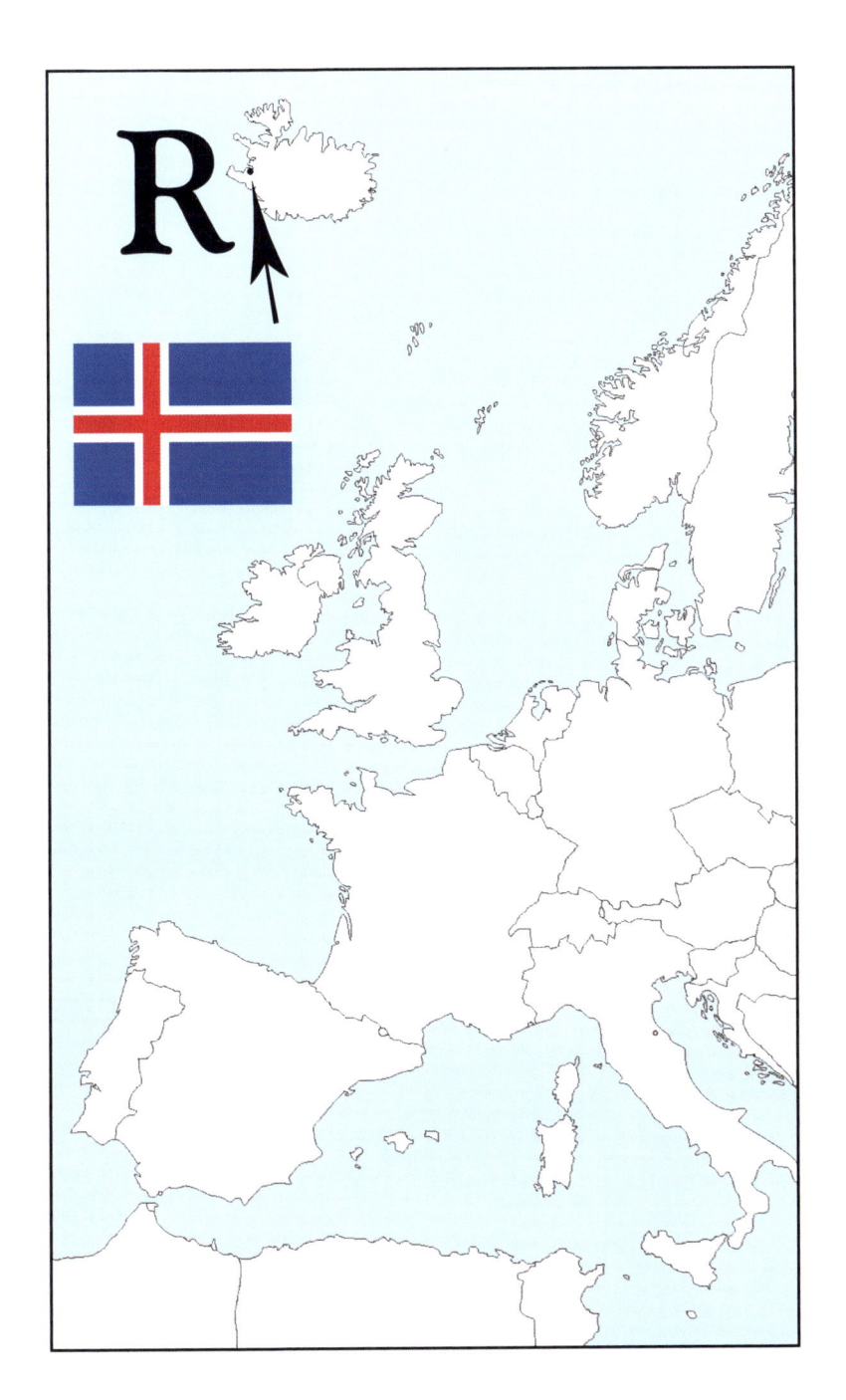

REYKJAVIK

Althing's for all men?

I'd always thought Iceland must be a fascinating place, and I'd love to go there. The chance came when it was announced that the Progressive Party – Iceland's Liberals – had invited the British Liberals to send an official delegation to meet them for an exchange of views and a general chewing of the fat. It would be led by our party leader in the Lords, Viscount Thurso, and ordinary party members interested in going – at their own expense, of course – were invited to apply. Two German FDP (Free Democrat) MPs, representing Bremen and Bremerhaven, joined us for the visit.

It was going to be more or less a long weekend, extending into the beginning of what was, luckily, half-term at my school. But I would have to have Friday afternoon off in order to join the rest of the delegation and catch the plane. I rang the Education Office in Winchester and explained what it was I wanted to do, and would they be prepared to give me half a day's leave of absence so that I could take the opportunity of a lifetime. No problem, they said, but you'll have to clear it with the Head.

Most headmasters, you might think, would be perfectly happy to indulge one of their senior staff who requested a half-day, on top of which the afternoon I wanted off was the end of the week preceding half-term and the school is winding down in preparation for the break. The actual cover I was asking for amounted, in fact, to just two lessons as I was free the other two. I canvassed my colleagues to arrange cover, and easily found two willing to help me out. But the Head refused me permission unless the LEA paid for a supply teacher to cover for me. When I relayed this to the Education Office they just laughed. Pay for supply cover for two lessons? No way. The Head dug his heels in, and kept me dangling until the middle of the week itself before accepting that the LEA was not going to give him a supply teacher and as they'd granted me formal permission he'd have to give way and let me go. Thanks, for nothing. I've been at the school for fifteen years, I'm in charge of pastoral care for 250 kids, but there's bugger-all pastoral care for me when I seek it. But that was the sort of man he was, as he showed many times in the way he treated his staff, though this is not the place to go into details.

I noticed two strange things about Reykjavik. One, there were no chimneys. Buildings are heated by hot water from deep underground, due to having geysers. Two, there were no dogs. I later asked a local why this was.

He asked in response, 'What do dogs eat?'

'Er, meat.'

'We have practically no meat in Iceland. We just have sheep, so apart from lamb it all has to be imported. Why should we spend our hard-earned foreign currency on importing meat just to feed it to dogs? You can have a cat – cats eat fish, and we have plenty of that!'

Apparently the only dogs allowed were working dogs on farms, and I presumed guide dogs for blind people – though I didn't see any.

As an official British delegation we were invited to a reception at the British Embassy, which turned into something of a memorable occasion. The ambassador was immensely tall and immensely thin, and had a passion for Gilbert & Sullivan. After a few drinks one of his staff sat down at the piano and we began a sing-song. In my student days I did four Gilbert & Sullivan productions in four years – my credits include Col Fairfax in *The Yeomen of the Guard* and Cox in *Cox and Box* – and I ended up singing duets with the ambassador while we all gradually got a skin-full out of his hospitality budget. Finally the evening ended, and as he'd had rather more to drink than intended he asked us to escort him back to his residence. That explained how two official delegates from the Liberal Party ended up staggering through the streets of Reykjavik in pitch darkness, trying desperately to hold the ambassador upright while all three of us singing chunks of *The Mikado* at the tops of our voices. It was just as well that his residence wasn't far and we didn't encounter any of the local constabulary.

A couple of other observations at that time may be of interest.

It was March, but still cold and dark much of the day. Yet I saw a bunch of boys in shorts and football shirts playing football on a cinder pitch in the near-freezing gloom, and marvelled at their hardiness. Perhaps being descended from Vikings? Then it was the hail – *horizontal!* I've never either before or since experienced hail which comes straight at you full in the moosh. No wonder the lads playing football were so tough. Wouldn't have survived otherwise.

The serious part of the visit was talking to Icelandic politicians, who took us to witness a session of their parliament, the *Althing*. But there was also time for some sight-seeing, so we were taken to see a geyser which although closed out of season was specially opened up for us. It spewed boiling water from a depth of, if I remember correctly, about 5000 feet, and could be timed exactly to one spout every twenty seconds – with a wet mark on the ground where the water came down, so watch out not to stand there as you'd get scalded. They also took us to see Gullfoss, perhaps the most famous waterfall in Iceland, and standing on a ledge immediately beneath the cascade I was able to stick my hand up into the torrent as it came over the ledge, but in perfect safety (unless you slipped and fell, in which case . . .).

Icelanders are immensely proud of their claim that the *Althing*

first met in the open air at Thingvellir in 930, nowadays the most sacred site in the country, and is the oldest democratic parliament in the world. 'But we English were first as a result of holding King John over a barrel in 1215!' you may cry. Well, maybe. The definition of 'Mother of Parliaments' depends on whether you base the claim on earliest foundation, in which case the Icelanders win by about three centuries, or continuity, in which case we do. The *Althing* was suppressed by the Norwegians at the start of their colonial occupation during the Middle Ages, and wasn't resurrected until 1843. Our parliament, although set up almost exactly at the time the *Althing* was suppressed, has had a continuous existence from that time.

The *Althing* is housed in a rather undistinguished detached building, with a door opening straight onto the street and no signs of security whatever. Visitors go up a broad, red-carpeted stair to the second floor, whence they can look down on the proceedings below. The feeling of being in the Upper Circle in a theatre is reinforced by the fact that the couple of dozen seats for the public are arranged in three tiers, while on the left-hand side of the chamber below are a pair of double doors reaching from floor to

Thingvellir, the ancient meeting place of the Althing!

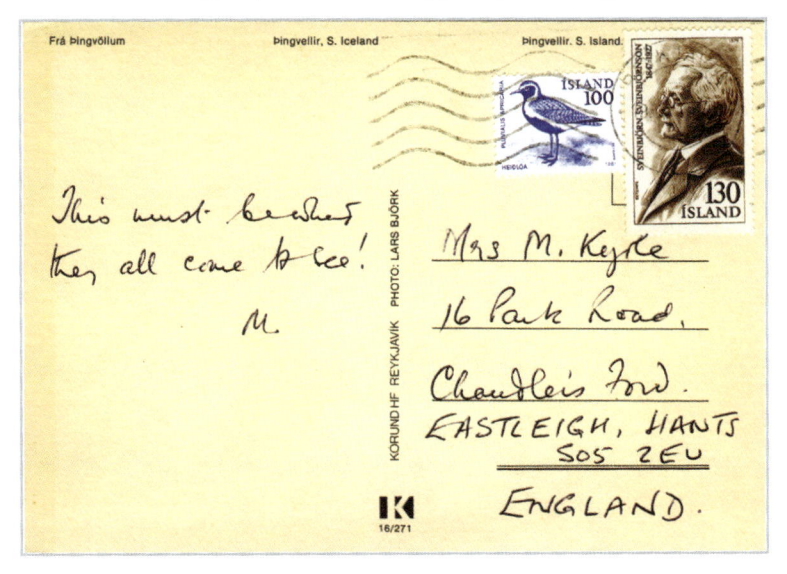

ceiling which open into another room.
  'What's that?' I asked.
  'That's the Upper House', I was told.

The *Althing* comprises 60 members, all elected together. From these 60 they elect 20 to form the Upper House, and the remaining 40 make up the Lower House. While debate was continuing in the Lower House, officials bearing papers passed between the two chambers, the immense doors opening silently and closing equally silently behind them. The chairman (Speaker?) sat on a raised chair facing the members, but behind him were ordinary windows with plain glass through which one could clearly see pedestrians in the street outside, walking past without a second glance. There appeared to be no police on duty, no armed guards, nothing. And as the debate proceeded no one so much as raised his voice. A marked contrast with the yah-ing and boo-ing which passes for acceptable conduct in our House of Commons. One wonders if the original was conducted in such measured tones back in the tenth century – 'No battleaxes, and all helmets to be left in the sheep pen' – perhaps?

We tend to think of Iceland as a European country, but in fact it's mid-Atlantic. OK, the people are of European stock, a mixture of Norsemen and Celts, but for centuries they were deliberately cut off from the rest of the world first by the kings of Norway who ruled Iceland from 1262 until 1380, and then when Norway lost its independence and became part of a joint realm ruled by the King of Denmark the Danes continued the embargo. Trade with Iceland was a royal monopoly from 1602, was slightly relaxed in 1787 to allow any subject of the Danish crown to trade but it wasn't until 1854 that commerce was opened up to all-comers. Denmark granted home rule in 1904, and independence under the crown in 1918. Only in 1944 did Iceland became a totally independent republic.

My brief visit taught me that for a country 80% of whose economy is dependent on a single product, fish, the so-called 'cod wars', after Iceland unilaterally extended its fishing limits to 200 miles in 1975 and British and Icelandic vessels squared up to each other and threatened violence in defence of fishing rights, may have been merely a sideshow to us but for them had been a matter of national survival. If countries aren't allowed to manage their local resources to sustain their population, how can we expect them to be peaceful neighbours and how do we expect to spread prosperity? Are Third World countries poor because they have no assets, or poor because what assets they have are exploited or plundered by First World countries which have bigger financial clout or more developed technology? But as examining that problem in depth will keep you awake all night, let's leave it for now. You can mull it over with your breakfast egg tomorrow.

March 1982

POSTSCRIPT
A dolphin was ostracised by the rest of his pod for mating with another species.
He protested that it was unintentional, an accident.
'That was no accident,' the other dolphins replied. 'You did it on porpoise.'

Goodnight.

S

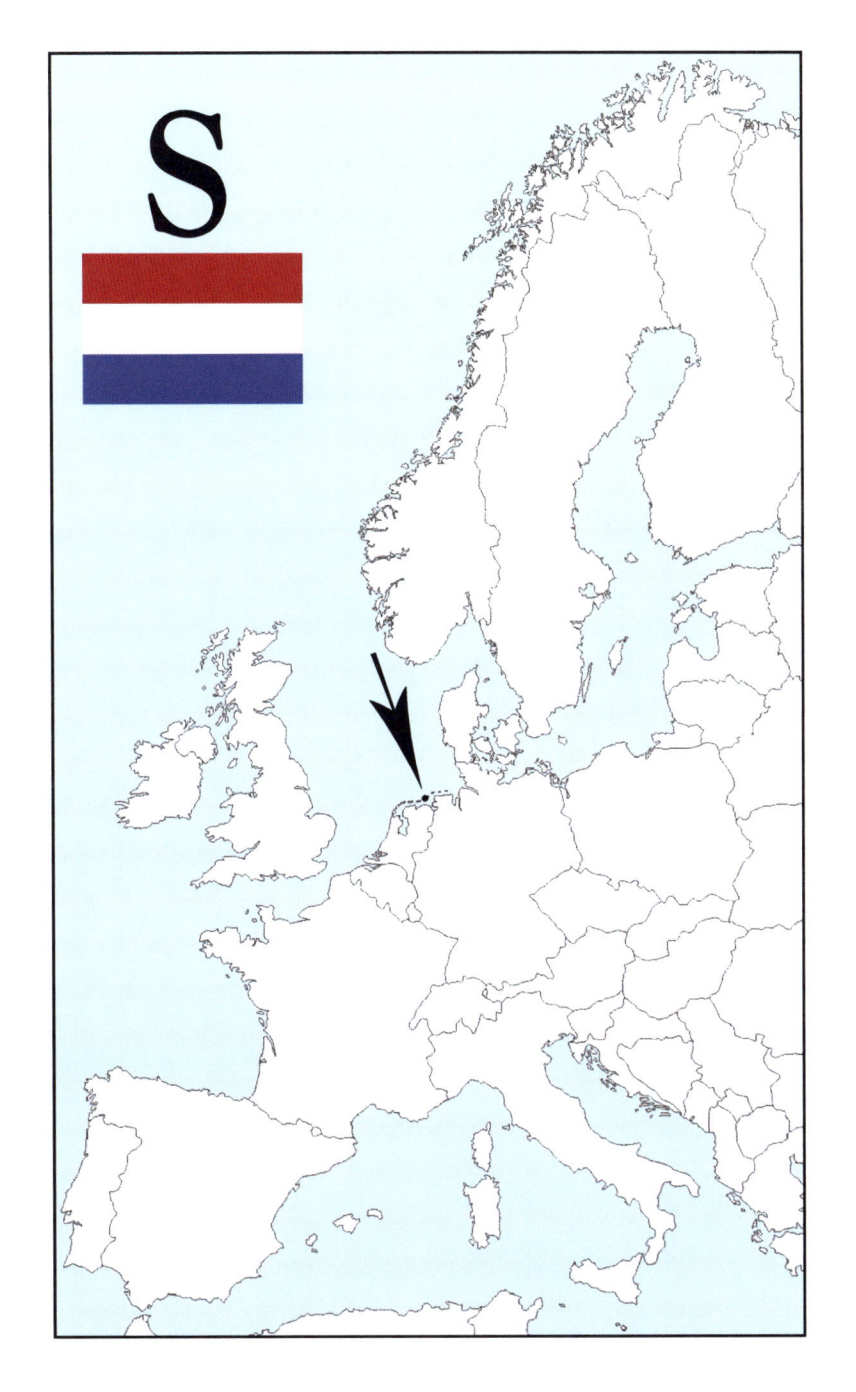

SCHIERMONNIKOOG
BUS BOOT BUS

Vervoer met de bus naar Lauwersoog vv. Lauwersoog-Schiermonnikoog vv. Vervoer met de bus op het eiland (uitsluitend vanaf de boot naar uw bestemming vv).

Stempel heenreis

Stempel terugreis

ARRIVA   WAGENBORG   NoordNed

Groningen

N° 300577

AR 05-40

SCHIERMONNIKOOG

Schier delight!

One of the reasons few English people go to Schiermonnikoog is that they can't pronounce it – 'I want a ticket to... er, Seer, Skeer, Sheer' and by that point you've forgotten the rest of the name anyway. If you know not, it's usually described as the smallest inhabited of the Dutch Frisian Islands (it depends on the state of the tides when you measure it). Farther to the east lies even smaller Rottumeroog, a wildlife sanctuary, and then it's the border so other islands beyond and in some cases smaller belong to Germany.

Furthering my mildly sustained ambition of visiting them all, I asked Danny, my Dutch friend whom I've known since childhood (hers) and who lives in Amsterdam, to fix us a short break. We were coming over to attend her retirement party (*another story – you'll have to wait*), and being the right time of year it would be an opportunity to knock off another island. She fix.

Getting there is complicated. Danny doesn't drive, so it's public transport. Nothing wrong with the rail system in the Netherlands, although the locals complain all the time. But from Amsterdam you have to reach the far north of the country, which means finding a train to Groningen, and you come up against the first hurdle if you're not with a Dutch speaker because it looks like one thing in English but sounds quite different when the Dutch say it. It doesn't begin with a hard 'g' as you would expect – especially if you have a smattering of German – but with a guttural 'ch' as in the Scottish way of pronouncing 'loch'. Easy enough when you know, but an elephant trap when no one's warned you. Then there is the Dutch habit of not pronouncing the final 'n', so the town's name ends with an unstressed vowel, 'uh'. The result is something like 'Hroninga'. None of this mattered to me, as Danny was doing the talking. But it shows the obstacles facing an unaccompanied English speaker trying to get to such a destination. And if instead of via Groningen you opted for the alternative, slightly more direct, route, that means going via Leeuwarden – and try pronouncing *that!*

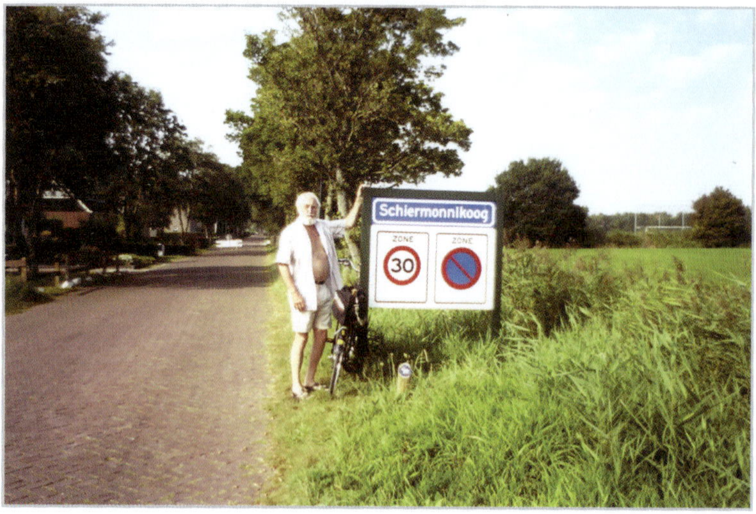
Schiermonnikoog
ZONE
30
ZONE

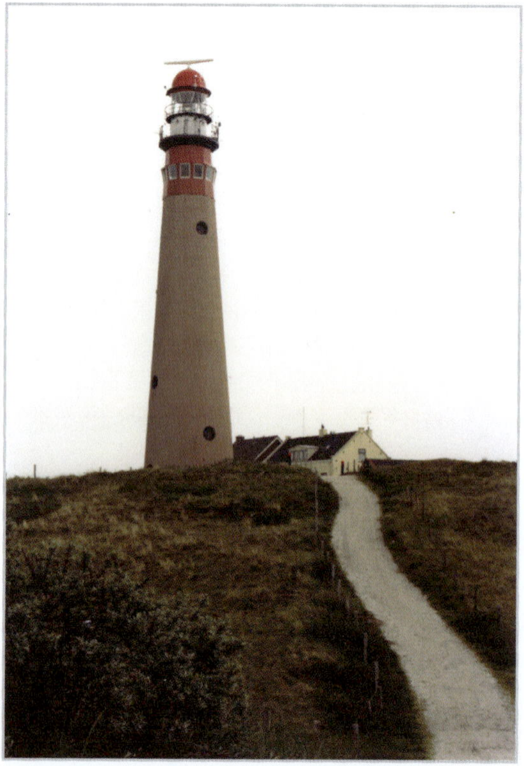

In fact, Danny had planned to go via the said Leeuwarden, but the train was delayed somewhere near Amersfoort for no obvious reason – it just stopped in the middle of nowhere, and there was no announcement – and when we got off at Leeuwarden we'd missed the connecting bus. Nothing for it but have some lunch in the station buffet, an enormous cavern whose walls were decorated with art from the great days of the railways at the end of the nineteenth century when they were all the rage and were opening up parts of the country which hitherto had been backwaters but were now able to join the mainstream and develop. We caught the next available train on to Groningen, where we'd pick up the bus to Lauwersoog, whence the ferry leaves for Schiermonnikoog. The bus leaves from right outside the railway station, but we found even the locals were having trouble making sense of the timetable and eventually Danny worked out that we'd missed it by ten minutes and the next one didn't leave for two hours.

But a temporary disaster can have an upside: we had two hours to kill and that gave us time to walk into the town centre and admire the architecture of the provincial capital. Well worth it, and I look forward to spending some time there at some future date and seeing the inside of some of the buildings I only had time to see the outside of. Back to the bus terminus, get on, relax and enjoy the countryside on the way to the coast and link up with the ferry. It's only a tiny island, so a rowing boat, perhaps? A flat-bottomed barge run on paraffin? No way – the ferry is absolutely enormous, as it has to take lorries to supply the islanders with every necessity.

The ferry terminal on Schiermonnikoog is right at the eastern tip, obviously built on reclaimed land for the sole purpose of providing a berth for the huge vessel. In former times, one supposes, people travelled in smaller boats which could tie up alongside a wall as they do in Vlieland, and before that you sailed as close inshore as you could get, avoiding the treacherous mudflats and sandbanks, and got off and waded ashore. The buses and taxis were waiting, and our bus had a scheduled stop right outside our hotel.

For so small an island, it is remarkably diverse. Next morning we walked down the road to the nearest cycle hire shop and within minutes were riding on the dedicated track through fields, then a small forest, then across water meadows where long-haired cattle grazed. The cattle, it appears, are the only means of keeping the land in good condition, as it floods in winter and because the ground is so soft no mechanical means exists to keep the grass down and the only possible alternative method is to leave cattle to roam free and graze it off. Walking off the tracks can be a bit risky, as there are muddy and boggy bits and in the wetter times of year you could find yourself in real trouble and all that's left of you on the surface is your hat and a few bubbles.

We reached the edge of the beach, which stretched out of sight in either direction and it was perhaps a quarter of a mile from the water's edge to where we had to leave our bikes. The water was ridiculously shallow, so much so that the only way to get wet was to sit down or lie down and let the gentle breakers wash over you. But the currents in deeper water are lethal, and there were explanatory notices and flags flying warning visitors not to be tempted to go out of their depth to swim except at certain states of the tide. After all, this is not the beach in some sandy cove – it's the North Sea out there. Far out on the horizon were several beacons on platforms, and while we bathed or enjoyed a snack we could observe the periodic flashes of their beams and the passing ships which depended on them for safe navigation in what by any standards is a very dangerous stretch of water.

Danny thought the sea too cold to go right in, but I managed it if only to be able to tell Margaret when we got back that I had. 'We British', and all that. No, she wasn't with us. Why? A heat wave was forecast, and she's not good in heat (I said '*in*', not '*on*') and waived the trip. 'Go without me', she insisted. 'I'll cat-sit.' That was an extremely brave decision, not only because she actually didn't much like cats but also because Danny's cat, Pinguin, is worth a story in his own right, as, indeed, are several of her previous animals. Fierce, unpredictable, noisy and determined – some might say psychotic – how glad we all were that a previous owner had had his claws removed. We suspected he was a reincarnation, but were not sure what of. At five o'clock one morning we'd been woken by a thud on the door of our bedroom. Pinguin, determined to join us in bed, was shoulder-charging it.

The island's name is derived from Old Dutch 'schier' – 'grey', the word for a monk – 'monnik', and the Fris word 'oog' which means an island. In the fourteenth century the island came into the possession of the Cistercian monastery of Klaarkamp in Friesland, who sent some of their order – the Grey Friars – to see if their new acquisition had any economic value. Some farming people were brought in and gradually a small community grew up, supporting themselves and the monks who lived on the island by raising cattle for meat, milk and cheese and giving an income and some meagre profit to send back to the mother house. As in England after the Dissolution of the Monasteries in 1536 when Henry VIII sold off monastic land and the buildings themselves to anyone with the money to pay, similarly in 1580 staunchly Protestant Holland confiscated monastic property, and the island came into private ownership. Three centuries later in 1892 it was bought by a German aristocrat, but at the end of the Second World War in 1945 the Dutch government seized it as an 'enemy treasure' and it became once again the property of the Dutch state.

Een schierer monnik

The original inhabitants have since been joined by a goodly number of retirees, attracted by the tranquillity of the place. There are buses and private cars, but no one's in a hurry. Some houses proudly display on their facades the fact that they date from the eighteenth century, others are of more recent construction. Plenty of shops, bars and restaurants, and although tourism is important – hence the abundance of cycle hire – out of season there is a sufficiently large resident population to sustain a retail economy. And there's always the ferry to the mainland and a bus to Groningen or Leeuwarden if you want a day out and a visit to the big stores but don't want to take your car.

September 2005

POSTSCRIPT
A sardine with her family were swimming along when a submarine passed above them.
Baby sardine: 'Mummy, what's that?'
Mummy sardine: 'That, darling, is a tin of men.'

Goodnight.

T

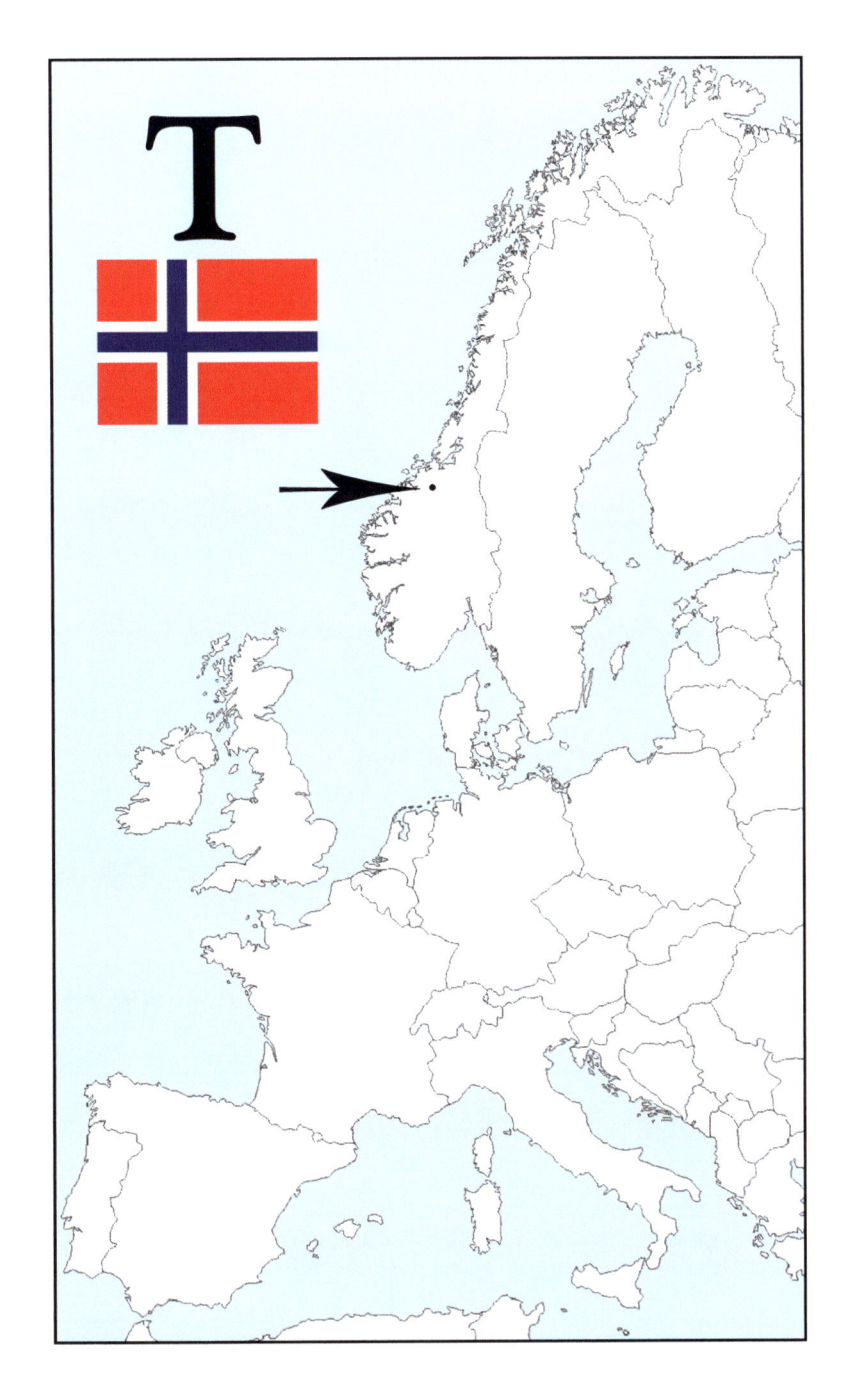

The Cathedral in Trondheim

TRONDHEIM

...the farther you go, the farther you still have *to go!*

This was the limit of the railway line from Oslo, and we were pretty knackered after the long train ride. 'We' on this occasion was Mike, who I still count as my best friend although we don't see much of each other. He had had a pretty roughshod childhood, his father having patented a battery-driven teaspoon and gone bankrupt trying the market it, and whose next invention – a half-size breadknife for when you only want to cut half a slice – was equally a failure. But I digress. From Trondheim north the only way is by road. As we soon discovered, after a time it wasn't road either, but track. Why spend public money putting a hard surface on a road which will break up in the winter and be impassable, and is hardly used in summer anyway? All serious transport of goods and people is by ship along the coast, and for hundreds of miles North Norway between the sea and the frontier with Sweden is so narrow that almost every settlement is either on the coast or within sight. Our aim was to get up to North Cape, so this was as far as we could get by public transport. We'd planned to hitchhike. Now we had no choice. We were barely one-third of the way. In fact, about 800 miles of not very much lay in front of us.

North Cape

We were relaxing in the Common Room of the youth hostel with our pipes well lit and on the lookout for company to pass the evening. One lad, as black as your hat and in consequence standing out a mile because everyone else in the hostel was a North European (which is hardly surprising, as we were *in* northern Europe) turned out to be from the Belgian Congo and like us a student thumbing his way around Europe during the vac. I'd never met anyone before from his country, and we soon lapsed into conversing in French as he found that easier than English. He was studying in Belgium (the colonial power at that time, so no wonder), and taking the opportunity to see a bit of the rest of the continent before going back home to take up his career in the capital of his own country, Léopoldville. The chap next to him was a Swede, but from not far away right up against the border and amazingly he had never before seen the sea! Even more amazing was that he said he'd never heard of Belgium and had absolutely no idea where it was. We wouldn't have been so surprised if he'd said he'd never heard of the Belgian *Congo* – but Belgium itself? Maybe Swedish education wasn't as enlightened or enlightening as we thought. The third member of our group was Anders, a native, whose English was so good I asked him if he was studying it at university.

'No,' he said. 'I'm studying physics at what you call A level.'

'So how come your English is so good?'

'All our textbooks are in English.'

'Why's that?'

'Well, think how many Norwegians there are (about 3 million), then think how many of them want to study physics to A level. Maybe a hundred altogether? It just isn't economic to print physics textbooks in Norwegian for so few people, and anyway anyone going on to university and taking a science degree will end up working either abroad or for a Norwegian firm which is engaged in research or trade with international partners, mainly in the US, or in import/export, and for any of that you have to have English because no one speaks Norwegian except us.'

Seemed to make sense.

Amongst other travellers with whom we fell into conversation

Hilsen fra Trondheim

A Sami family outside their tent

were a couple of canoeists who'd just returned from the Lofoten Islands, whose intriguing story about their journey and their experiences on the islands I related in the first book in this series, my *Little Green Nightbook*. Then there were a couple of Danes in their mid-twenties, one tall and thin and the other short and rotund – a sort of Laurel and Hardy in reverse. They were highly adventurous travellers who'd made it beyond the confines of Europe into North Africa, and had tales to tell about Morocco. On arrival in Casablanca they'd been warned of the ingeniousness and ruthless efficiency of the local thieves, evidenced by what befell a young German lad travelling alone who'd set up his tent on the beach with his rucksack, stove, sleeping bag and other necessaries arranged inside around him and who when he woke up next morning found himself lying on the sand in his pyjamas and that was all – everything else had been stolen.

Our two Danes explained that they had not been in the least put off by this story. 'We'll be fine', they'd said. 'We have a good Danish knife' (the speaker held his hands out about two feet apart, indicating just how big it had been). They proceeded to erect their tent out on the beach, stood their rucksacks side by side and when they got into their sleeping bags laid the knife on the ground between them – the slightest disturbance and either of them could reach out, grab it and confront the intruder. And it worked. Next morning they were still safely cocooned in their sleeping bags inside their tent and all their gear was just as they'd left it when they turned in.

Except for the knife, which had gone.

Moroccan Thieves 1, *Danes* nil.

The weather was very hot and sunny, and after looking round the city and its cathedral we found a deserted rocky beach where we could strip off, laze in the sun, read the copy of *The Observer* which we'd found at a newsstand and perhaps have a dip. Not expecting hot weather in North Norway we hadn't brought such luxury items as bathing trunks as it would be yet another thing to carry and hardly likely to get used. Mike, stark naked, jumped into the water, but after just a few seconds of delighted squeals leapt out again even more quickly – Trondheim Fjord is fed by melt water off glaciers inland and their low temperature doesn't encourage total immersion. Norwegian waters are serious matters, and not to be trifled with by 'occasional' bathers. It wasn't too bad in water up to the knees, and I myself was not in the least tempted to go in any farther, knowing that we were a lot farther north than either of us had ever been before and way beyond the northernmost parts of Great Britain. But as we lay starkers on the rocks enjoying the sun, suddenly we heard women's voices. A group of what looked from the distance like office typists out for their lunch break were coming along the beach towards us! We had no desire to end up in custody at the local cop shop for exposing ourselves, but the problem was that we were lying on the rocks and our clothes were twenty feet away on the beach and any attempted movement involving sliding off the rocks to reach them would mean we'd be spotted. So we tried to shrink ourselves down as flat as we could and just hope they wouldn't look up and spot us, holding our breath as the girls walked by oblivious of the fact that there were two naked young men only a few feet away. You have to picture us bollock naked, trying to lie as flat as possible on top of a rock, keeping absolutely silent while holding our breath and our stomachs in and crossing our fingers. That was us.

When someone asks me if I've ever had an embarrassing moment, I say 'Nearly'.

August 1959

POSTSCRIPT
Customer: 'I'd like to buy a new armchair.'
Assistant: 'Certainly, sir. What colour would you like?'
Customer: 'I'd like one to match my eyes.'
Assistant: 'I'm sorry, sir. I don't think we have any bloodshot armchairs.'

Goodnight.

U

183

ULAN BATOR

Bator late than never?

Looking at landlocked Mongolia on a map, I always reckoned it amongst the least likely places I'd ever visit. However, planning a holiday partly around Lake Baikal put me near enough to consider popping over the border to tick another box. Then a second thought struck me: having got so far, what's the point of just 'popping over the border' and then getting back onto the Trans-Siberian Railway? Having reached Mongolia, it's daft not to spend at least a few days exploring it. The opportunity won't come again.

The country is about the size of Western Europe yet has only some three million people, and of these one million live in Ulaanbaatar (the double letters indicate where the stress goes). It's known by the locals simply as 'UB'. Mention Mongolia to most people and they have only one thought: Genghis Khan. They vaguely remember that in the Middle Ages he led the Mongols on a rampage across Central Asia and reached the frontiers of Europe, destroying everything in his way and on his way.

In real life, I'm not sure I'd have turned my back on him!

Modern Mongolians take a different view, and the huge statue of Chinggis Khaan (their spelling) in front of their Parliament Building says it all. He's seen as a national hero, the 'father of the nation' who united the nomadic Mongols for the first time at the end of the 12th century and created the largest land empire the world has ever seen. And he only destroyed those who opposed him. Those who submitted were allowed to keep their own customs and religion – a degree of toleration which was certainly not found in contemporary Christian Europe where Jews were persecuted and heretics routinely put to death and often in particularly nasty ways.

Arriving by train from Russia, we – Mike (remember Narvik?) and I – headed straight out to a country park 70kms north-east for a few days living in a traditional nomadic *ger* (*pron. 'grrrr'*) and experiencing a bit of rural life (*which I'll tell you about under another letter – but in another book*). Once outside the city limits tarmac ceased, and the road thereafter was of indeterminate and inconsistent width because it had no proper edge and drivers wishing to avoid a vast pothole or vertiginous rut just left the road, thus in the process increasing its width. As well as lacking any kind of kerb, the road across country was also devoid of a consistent surface, any lines indicating where the middle was supposed to be or any traffic directions, signage or lighting.

Returning two days later, our driver seemed to be fleeing a wolf pack, so fiercely did he steer us around the world-class ruts and potholes. When we reached the city limits we had to go through a toll and pay 500 *tugriks* (the local currency, and worth about 20p in our money), which is apparently charged on all vehicles. With this additional income, you'd expect the city fathers to maintain the roads within the city to a higher standard than in the countryside. But no, hardly any difference until well into the city centre; not so many ruts, but still a plentiful supply of potholes. There were plenty of traffic police fighting a losing battle, with – a surprise – the word 'POLICE' across the back of their luminous jackets – just like that, i.e. in English. As well as being surprised that they use the English word and not whatever it is in their own language, on top of that Mongolian isn't written in Latin script but a slightly adapted version of Cyrillic despite not being a Slavonic language.

Our tour of the city began with paying our respects to Chinggis Khaan and visiting the museum devoted to his times, which contained some interesting coins from the Early Middle Ages and banners carried by armies when approaching a town to show whether they came in peace (a white banner) or meant war (a black one). Then to the Gandan monastery, thronged with devotees buying bags of nuts from street vendors to feed to the hundreds of pigeons who knew which side their bread was buttered – so to speak. Coo! *(Sorry!)*. There are plans to re-locate to a new site some 50km distant, and to erect a statue of the Buddha which will be taller than the Statue of Liberty. A model of his foot was displayed on a plinth, giving some idea of just how colossal the final statue will be.

After lunch in a Mongolian barbecue our guide took us to the memorial to Russian-Mongolian friendship and to those who died during the Second World War, erected at the top of Zaisan Hill requiring visitors to climb several hundred steep steps. It's very obvious that the architects and painters were strongly influenced by the concept of socialist realism, but in this instance it has worked incredibly well – even allowing for the element of propaganda contained in a succession of portraits depicting sturdy, good-looking men and women and every uniform smart and ready for a march past. We had an interesting encounter there with a young Chinese couple talking to each other in English. When questioned, they explained that they'd met on the train. The young man was from Hong Kong and didn't speak very good Mandarin, and the girl was from south-east China and couldn't understand his Cantonese – so they decided that as they'd both studied in Britain it was easier to talk to each other in English than struggle to communicate using two different versions of Chinese. An interesting example of the dominance of English as the world's *lingua franca* that two educated Chinese opt to use it.

Until the twentieth century the Mongols remained a largely nomadic people, even moving their capital – known at that time as Urga – with them. They were conquered by the Chinese in 1691, but when the Manchu dynasty fell in 1911 they declared their independence and turned to their religious leader, the lama Bogd Khan. His palace, built between 1893 and 1903, is open to tourists, and the interiors are well kept and full of examples of Buddhist art, calligraphy and especially *thangkas*; but while the skill and devotion of the artists are not to be doubted the fact is that the displays are largely meaningless to a viewer unfamiliar with the intricacies and symbolism of Buddhist belief.

The open spaces between the buildings, on the other hand, are surprisingly unkempt. Bogd Khan agreed to become king, and even agreed to take a wife so that the people could have a queen. His throne is on display in the audience chamber, replete with 28 cushions representing the 28 provinces of Mongolia, and the seats where religious and lay officials sat. Ten years later he accepted constitutional limitations to his power, but when he died in 1924 the Communists took over and set up a dictatorship in imitation of what was happening at that time in their vast northern neighbour, Russia, and became to all intents and purposes a Soviet satellite. As we all know, the Soviet Union broke up in the 1990s and Belarus, Ukraine, the Baltic States and much of Central Asia became independent republics. It is less well known that at the same time the Mongolians threw off the Communist yoke and set about building a functioning democracy.

The cultural highlight of our visit was a performance of traditional Mongolian music and dance by a small, predominantly young, professional troupe who, dressed in elaborate costumes and quick-changing between acts amazed us with their dexterity on various traditional instruments and the obvious command of their repertoire – including the world-renowned local eccentricity, 'throat singing' (*hoomii* in Mongolian). Our guide said the show was staged between six and seven every night, and was essentially for tourists. But who can forget a contortionist who starts her act by standing on her right leg with her left leg at 180° with her knee against her ear – and as her finale sticks a peg in the floor, grips the top in her teeth and proceeds to perform a slow-motion head-stand!

On our final afternoon we popped along to the post office to get some stamps to post cards to friends and family, not having done so during our month in Russia prior to arriving in Mongolia. We'd been advised that they also stocked a wide range of souvenirs, and at keen prices. The problem in most cases was: the items didn't have any prices on them, so we had to keep asking one of the staff to show us each item and tell us how much it was. The next process was to tot up the total for multiple purchases and mentally convert the price in *tugriks* into sterling at 2200 to the £ – not the easiest of calculations to make in your head! While we're doing the mental arithmetic bit and debating the merits of this item or that, the assistant is standing holding the various items, eyes glazing over in boredom as she gazes into the middle distance. We then discovered – to our amazement – that in a shop geared up to accommodate foreign visitors and where all the serving staff spoke English they did not accept credit cards! So we had to go to the cashpoint, draw out the money, go and pay, take the goods (no wrapping paper or bags offered – the implication being 'You've bought it. Here it is. Take it away.') – and then if you decide you'd like something else go back and draw out more money and go through the whole rigmarole again. One of my additional purchases cost 2000 *tugriks*, which when I got my credit card statement back in England showed I'd been charged 92p for the currency and a £2 handling fee for withdrawing it!

This 5 tugrik note is worth approx. one-fifth of 1p!

Ulan Bator today is a thoroughly modern city, and its traffic jams bear comparison with the rush hour in any large conurbation – except that it has them all day long! From our hotel room on the 9th floor I could see a dozen cranes and as many half-built tower blocks, a clear indication of the influx of people into the city and the need to accommodate them. So it may not be beautiful – no 'old quarter' of the sort so keenly sought out by Western visitors to towns in foreign countries. But vibrant it sure is, and the smile on Chinggis Khaan's face doubtless indicates satisfaction with the modern Mongolia created by his descendants.

September 2012

POSTSCRIPT
The most remarkable slow bowler in cricket's history was so slow he could keep wicket off his own bowling.

Goodnight.

V

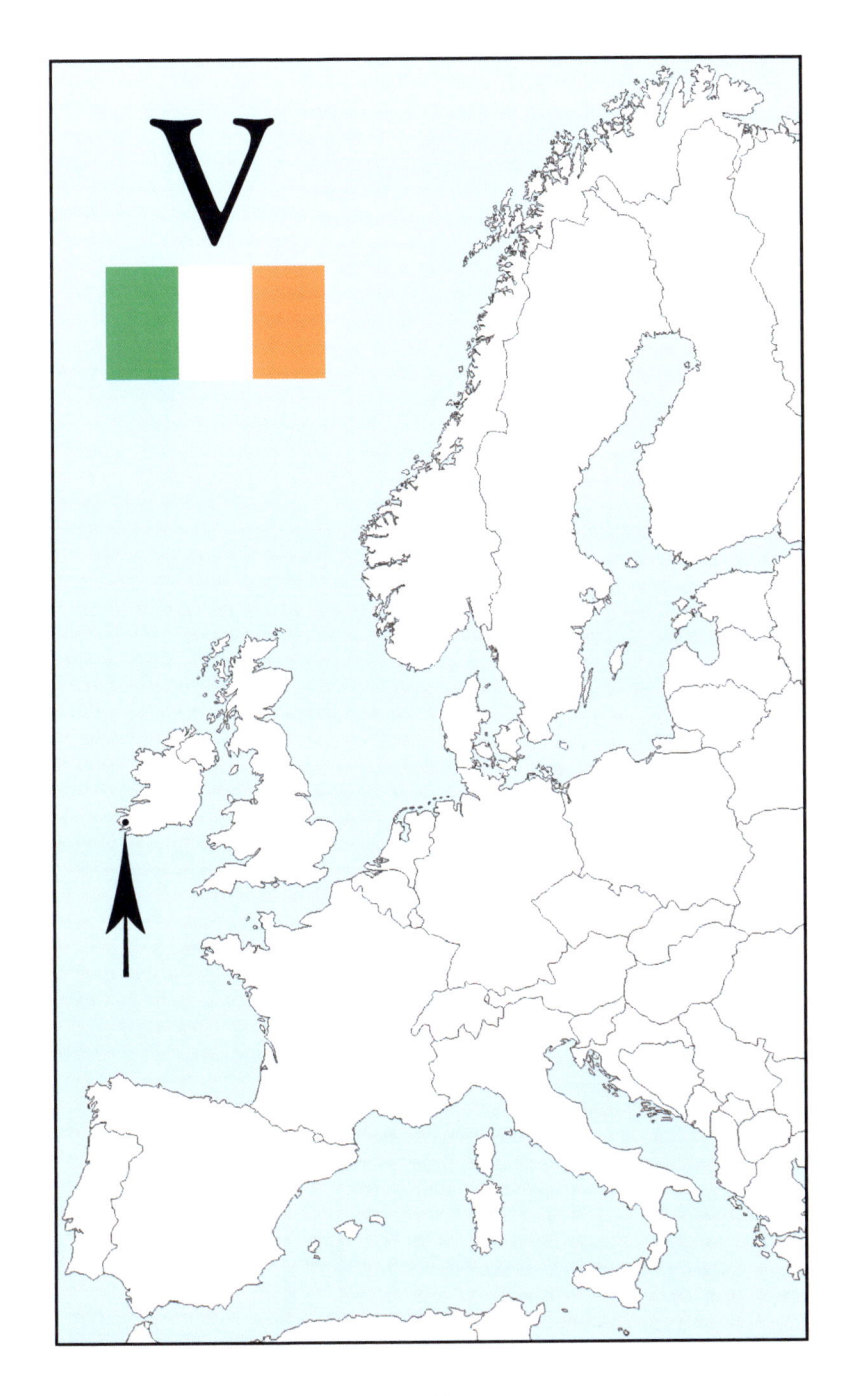

VALENTIA

Plan B to the end of the world

We arrived on schedule on the island, one of the departure points for boat trips out to The Skelligs. For those who don't know, these tiny islets lie off the coast of Kerry in the far south-west of Ireland.

Why go there?

For some four centuries up to about 1200 the larger islet, Skellig Michael, was the site of one of the most remote monastic communities in Christendom, where an abbot and twelve monks maintained their isolation from the temptations of the world by perching themselves on the top of a rocky outcrop which rises almost sheer some 700 feet above the sea, lashed by gales and most of the time inaccessible. They lie 8 miles out in the Atlantic – the farthest western point in the British Isles. There is a lighthouse. The next piece of land to the west is America.

We were booked into a B&B on Valentia where our host, who worked during the day at the Irish meteorological station on the island, informed us that due to adverse weather conditions no boats had ventured out to the Skelligs for a week and many visitors who had come intent on making the trip had run out of time and had had to go home disappointed. The boatmen stand with binoculars on various headlands and look at the landing stage on the island, and can tell through experience whether the height of the Atlantic swell is too great to permit landing. If it's too rough and no passengers could get ashore, there's no point in going.

We were, however, in luck. The very next day the weather moderated.

Down to the embarkation point, park the car and get aboard. The boat was tiny and completely open, and seemed quite inadequate for an eight mile voyage straight out into the Atlantic. But in the days of the monastery the monks used to make the trip in a coracle to fetch supplies or collect a novice or two. I guess they must have had supreme confidence in the power of prayer.

The weather may have moderated, but it was still blowing quite

Eight miles out into the Atlantic in this!

hard and obviously we were in for a bumpy ride. Plan B, then: get on first, sit with your back against the wheelhouse and be out of the wind. The other passengers ranged themselves on the benches around the gunwales, backs to the sea and exposed to wind and spray. It was a case, I observed to Margaret, of the operation of Jackson's Principle. What's that, you ask? There was, so it's said, a shipwrecked sailor who, as he reached safety at the top of the rope ladder slung over the side of the other ship, said to his rescuers, 'Pull the ladder up, Jack, I'm alright' – while many of his shipmates were still in the water. 'Jackson's Principle' is how Margaret and I describe the phrase *'I'm alright, Jack'*, a reference to people who are indescribably self-centred and whose only concern in life is themselves and their own convenience. *(You may start now, if you like, compiling a personal list. But be warned: it may keep you awake, so obviating the point of this being a 'Nightbook'!).*

However, it soon became evident that operating 'Jackson's Principle' had been, as Margaret usually put it when I did something right, *'one of my better ideas'*. The boat bounced about like a cork in the ocean swell, with a German girl being discretely sick over the side most of the way. We passed Little Skellig, a small but steep rock with no possible place to land, the haunt of seabirds and covered in guano *(OK – have it your way: bird shit)* . Not far now to the landing stage on Skellig Michael. This, apparently, had only been built comparatively recently, for the benefit of tourists. The monks had simply launched their coracles straight off the rocks into the water. But then, not very often and only in the calmest of sea conditions.

The way to the monastic ruins is up a long, winding flight of slightly fan-shaped steps cut into the bare rock and without any handrails or safety features – and a real clincher if you want an answer to that nagging question you've always been wondering about: 'Do I suffer from vertigo?'. Make no mistake – or rather, on the other hand, *make* a mistake – and it's non-stop straight into the *oggin* and that could be a couple of hundred feet straight down. Even in a moderate wind it's pretty scary, as the steps are constantly wet from spray. What it must be like in a gale hardly bears thinking about.

Onward and upward – and no handrail

At the top of the landing-stage the resident tour guides were there to greet us. The Irish Tourist Board, it appeared, employed three or four students to stay out on shifts of three weeks or so at a time to take visitors round the ruins and explain them. The top of the island has just about enough level ground to allow for the construction of a reservoir to catch rainwater, individual cells for the monks, a tiny chapel and to lay out an equally tiny kitchen garden. Life must have been incredibly hard – but then, that's what the monks wanted. According to their beliefs, the greater the privation on earth, the greater the purity of the soul and the greater the reward in heaven at the end.

A monk's 'bee-hive' cell

The guides told the story of Viking raiders who carried off the abbot, who ultimately starved to death. The small patch of level ground which constituted the monks' vegetable garden seemed hardly big enough to have supplied them with enough to eat, but presumably they caught fish and in any case were the sort of zealots who had chosen this spot for the ultimate experience in self-denial and would have eaten the barest minimum to stay alive. The ruins have been partially repaired, and our intrepid band of visitors wandered around them freely, taking photos. In particular, of the altar cross silhouetted against the east window. It had no glass. But then, had it ever?

How long visitors could stay depended on sea conditions, as it was essential to get back to the mainland – there's absolutely nowhere to stay on the island and no proper shelter. The guides have a hut but often no visitors for days at a time because no boats can reach them. Once the summer tourist season is over, the island is abandoned except for maintaining the lighthouse on the far side. Being a lighthouseman there must have been about the loneliest posting in the service one could have experienced.

We had the wind behind us on the return trip, which seemed to fill the skipper, a lad of about 17 judging by appearances, with such confidence that he abandoned the wheel and sat on the stern with his feet on the seating, backside sticking out over our wash, chatting to the nearest passengers. One untoward wave and he'd have done a backward somersault into the sea – leaving us adrift without a pilot. I was glad when we made harbour and tied up safely.

A visit to The Skelligs is the ultimate in tourism to remote parts so far as south-west Ireland is concerned, because even though the Great Blasket is equally difficult to reach it's a proper island where ordinary people once lived by farming and fishing, and some of the cottages abandoned when the last residents moved out in the 1930s have been taken over by new owners and renovated as summer retreats. No one has ever lived on The Skelligs except for the tiny medieval community of monks – and even they gave up in the thirteenth century. I could only marvel at their devotion and hardiness – and feel thankful that I had a welcoming B&B to get back to in Valentia and the prospect of a good dinner in a restaurant.

August 1990

POSTSCRIPT

Among the students in the University Dept. of Electrical Engineering were so many talented musicians that they formed their own orchestra. No one had the time to conduct full-time or so they appointed two to do it for half the year each. Each was, so to speak, a semi-conductor.

Goodnight.

W

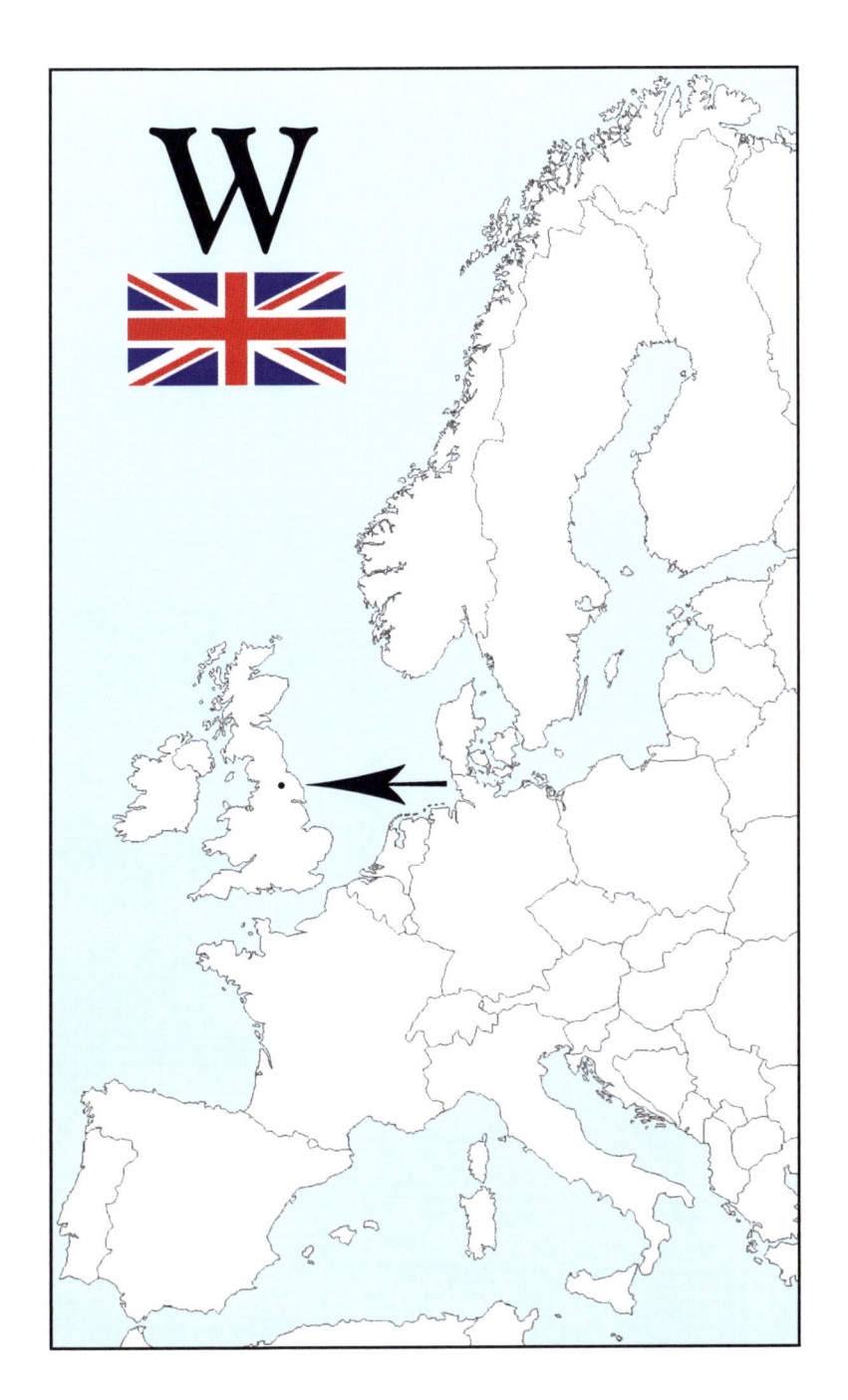

WETHERBY

As one life reaches its climax, two others begin

It was one hell of a dash. Mother's party was on Thursday, we had to get home and pack and be in Wetherby by late Friday ready for the wedding on Saturday – and it's a drive of 250 miles!

The run-up to Margaret's mother's hundredth birthday was long in the process and tough on the nerves – yes, it's pleasantly unusual to have your mother reach her century, but at the back of your mind is always the nagging fear that you'll have put in all this time and energy into making all the arrangements and then at the last minute she won't actually make it. It does happen. When I was mayor some twenty years ago I was all lined up to a present a bouquet of flowers to a lady whose 100th birthday was coming up, and she died the day before – leaving us with an expensive bouquet and no one to present it to. Very inconsiderate. Surely she could have just held on for another twenty-four hours, if only out of consideration for the council tax payers whose money she would be wasting by dying a day too soon?

The party itself went well, what with the local paper sending a photographer to the care home and all the residents joining in the celebratory drinks and nibbles. We all know that the Queen sends a card to people on their 100th birthday, but it's different when you actually see one. There are now so many people reaching three figures that it's hardly a phenomenon any longer, but in most families it's still a unique experience because whichever member of the family it is who's reached a hundred they are almost certainly the first one in *your* family to do so – however many others there are in other people's families up and down the country reaching the same milestone.

Ma enjoyed herself, and was more aware and alert than she'd been for months. She'd not been able to read for half-a-dozen years, and couldn't really even see the television. So what's the point of living if most of the time you're just sitting? You can't talk *all* the time, and frankly you run out of things to say. You can listen

I am so pleased to know that you are celebrating your one hundredth birthday on 19th May, 2011. I send my congratulations and best wishes to you on such a special occasion.

Elizabeth R

Mrs. Rita Round

to other people's conversation – but are you actually interested? Margaret spent a lot of time managing her affairs and visited every week, but it's a round trip of sixty miles across the New Forest and we had to be out by midday because that's when lunch is served and they wanted to get her downstairs into the dining room not only for the meal but also for a bit of company. Gave us the opportunity to investigate the menus of a whole host of country pubs all over the Forest (*arrangement: I pay for the petrol, you pay for the lunch*). But you're not back home till tea-time, so in effect visiting Mother took up a whole working day each week. Maybe not a problem if you have nothing else to do and no other responsibilities, but retired or not we both had busy lives and had to work round our other activities to find a day in the week when we could both be free to make the maternal visit. Can't go Saturday or Sunday – the A31 (the main road through the Forest to Bournemouth or the West Country) will be clogged with holiday traffic and likely as not we'll get stuck in a traffic tail-back. Monday's out – I've got a dentist appointment. Tuesday – no go, Margaret's got a meeting of the County Adoption Panel, and that takes all day. And she'll probably be so exhausted that she won't feel like visiting Mother on Wednesday. Etc., etc. Am I complaining? No. Just explaining.

Margaret was pretty knackered at the end of the party, what with reading out all the cards to Mother several times over, introducing all the family members, some of whom she hadn't seen for years, setting people up for group photos, liaising with the care home staff and regularly adjusting the transparent adhesive tape keeping her fixed smile in place. We got home, packed – posh clothes and lady's fancy titfer as well as usual holiday gear – and set the alarm for an early rise tomorrow.

The wedding was my younger nephew, Matthew, whose fiancée's family came from Yorkshire. We booked into a motel alongside the motorway, convenient for getting to the country house outside Wetherby where the ceremony would take place (no churches or religious element). It would also be convenient to get to anywhere else we fancied. Principally this would be York itself, which we both loved and wanted to re-visit and experience some of the major attractions again – possibly for the last time, as we're not likely to come this far north again. It would be interesting to see if the Jorvik Experience was still the same, and when we picked up a tourist brochure we read that there was a new medieval house to be explored, which had only been unearthed a couple of years previous when reconstruction work was undertaken and hidden walls were laid bare for the first time in five hundred years.

While in the North we also planned to take in some of the National Trust or English Heritage properties Margaret had always wanted to see but so far had not managed, in particular Bolsover Castle and the home of that extraordinary phenomenon Elizabeth, Countess of Shrewsbury, known as 'Bess of Hardwick': 'Hardwick Hall – more glass than wall', as it was dubbed at the time it was built during the reign of the first Elizabeth. Then there was Litchfield. We managed to find a space in a car park ideally placed for Margaret to take a photo of the famous twisted spire – only to find to her dismay that her camera battery was flat! Then to Knaresborough, where I sat for a moment on a bench in the main square next to an old boy dressed all in black and with a distinct frown on his face, but when I spoke to him he didn't answer so I didn't press him. There was a large wheel alongside him which he seemed to be guarding, so perhaps he was preoccupied with that.

The next day we made the journey to Bakewell, as I've been known to fancy a tart from time to time. The scenery is wonderful, and I made a mental note to come back another time and 'do' Derbyshire properly. The fly in the ointment with living on the south coast is that the attractions of the continent are just so close and the ferries so comfortable and so convenient if, like us, you have a penchant for French food and the pleasant scenery. It's less trouble for me to get to France than it is to get to the Midlands, and being as a result of many years of visiting pretty familiar with Normandy and Brittany and having a topped-up euro credit card in my pocket, it's naturally a first choice over driving a couple of hundred miles north to somewhere where I don't know the local geography when you've got a wife who's just as keen as you are to get stuck into an *assiette de fruits de mer*.

For the final drive home we managed to lose the road and ended up making a detour through countryside where we had no idea where we were but ended up – using the map – taking a cross-country route back to the main A1. In a particularly deserted section we found ourselves on a country road between the two main ones, looking for a lay-by to stop for a picnic. We parked facing a fence looking over a wide field system with a tractor working away in the far distance. On top of the fence posts local bird enthusiasts had nailed small upturned tins into which, presumably, they left titbits to encourage the local feathered wildlife to come, feed and be observed at close quarters – i.e. you parked close to the fence, stayed in the car, kept quiet and waited for the floor show. Several blackbirds arrived, clearly familiar with the scheme, and proceeded to start at one end of the fence, inspect the first tin and flutter on to the next before finally flying off in disgust (the tins were as it happened empty). But star of the show was a cock pheasant who sauntered across the road behind us as though he owned it (no hint of traffic sense whatever), flew nonchalantly up onto the top of the fence and proceeded to promenade majestically tightrope-style along the whole length investigating each tin in turn before finally dropping down on the other side of the fence and walking off in disgust – all the time apparently completely unaware that there were two humans watching his every move from barely ten feet away.

May 2011

POSTSCRIPT
A married couple in a rowing boat on a lake were having a fierce argument and ended up falling in the water. As they were brought ashore one of their rescuers asked them what had happened. 'We were having a row', said the husband. 'No, we weren't,' said the wife. 'We were having a row.'

Goodnight.

Y

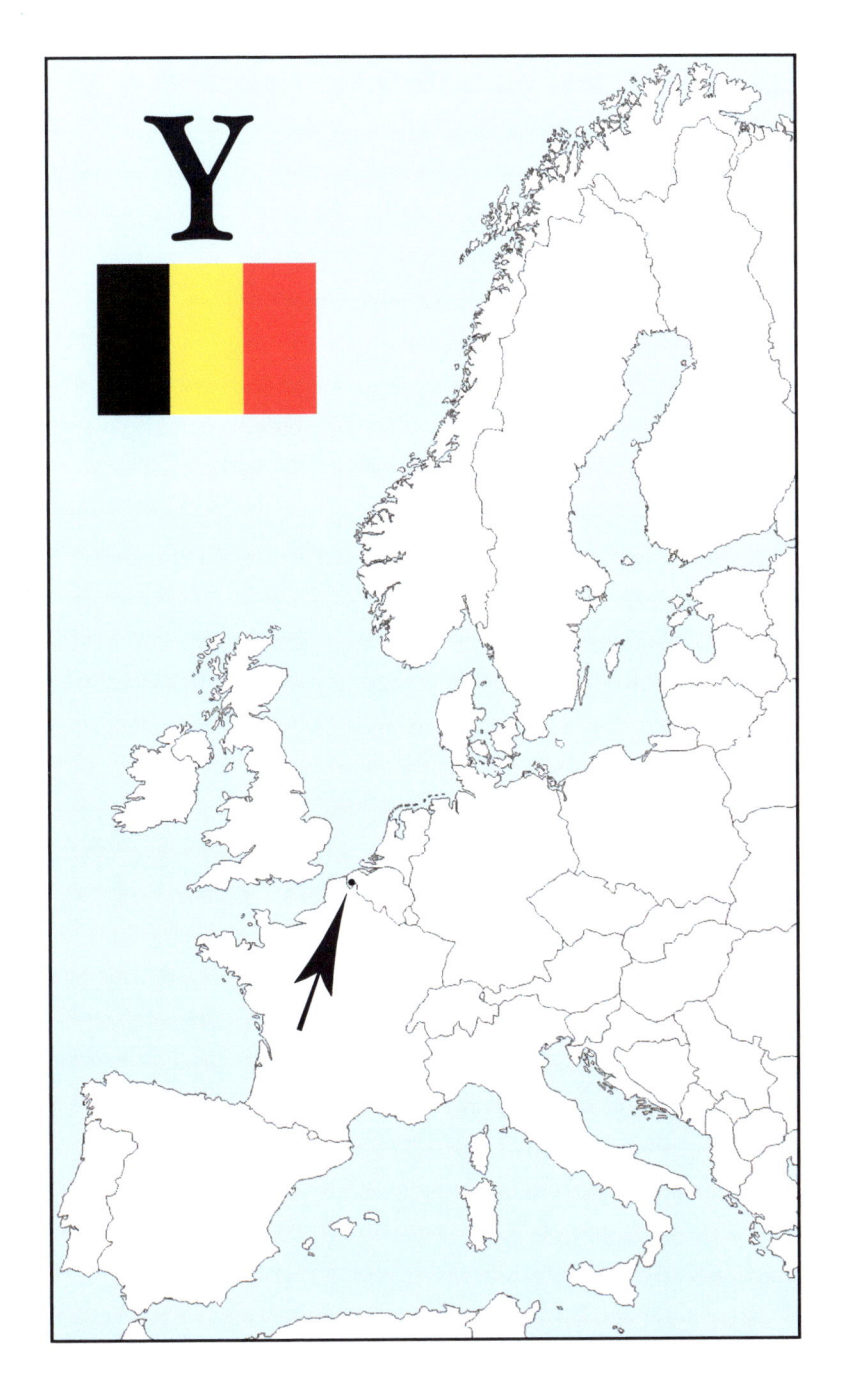

YPRES

Faith in the future

Ieper is much visited by the British, on account of the cemeteries and memorials to those who died in the First World War. Our visit was much more prosaic: a lunch stop on the way to the Channel Tunnel after a visit to the European Parliament in Brussels hosted by Chris Huhne, one of our MEPs.

Despite being a major centre of the wool trade in the Middle Ages, as were so many towns in Flanders, Ieper is not much visited, I think, by ordinary tourists interested in seeing something of Flemish history. They head for Bruges or Ghent. Maybe Antwerp. We've all learned in school that between 1914-18 Ypres was the site of not just one major battle but three, and we all know the Tommies called it 'Wipers' because seeing how it's spelled in French that was the way it looked as if it should be pronounced. We've all seen pictures of the devastation visited upon battlefield zones, how towns on the front line were reduced to rubble, and we just assume that postwar reconstruction was in 1920s architectural style, with modern public buildings, widened streets, art deco shopfronts if you're lucky and whatever the local equivalent was of council housing.

But the Flemings didn't do anything of the kind when rebuilding Ieper. They put it up again the way it was.

Parking our coach alongside the Cloth Hall, my first thought wasn't 'art deco' or 'concrete hangar' but my recollections of the Sukiennice in Kraków (built about the same time, too). I'm sure close inspection would reveal that the hall is a modern reconstruction, but from a casual glance just walking through it on the way to the main square and finding a restaurant it looks just like the original, begun in 1320, would have looked when completed. This is not deception big-time, it's recreating what was there, the way it was. It's about faith in the future. We lost a fine building in a war, but the war's over now, so let's have our history back.

The same attitude, I'm sure, inspired the Poles to rebuild the Old Town in Warsaw after the Second World War even though millions of people were homeless, starving, unemployed and suffering all manner of extreme economic and social hardship. But money was found for rebuilding the city's historic heart, painting it up and re-creating the town centre just as it had looked in the seventeenth century – emphasis on 'looked'. The interiors were built to modern standards in terms of ceiling heights (we're generally taller than our ancestors) and modern plumbing, electric lighting and fire exits, but façade as near as possible a carbon copy of what was originally constructed four centuries earlier. If Poland were to recover, it needed also to recover its history – so, I'm sure, must have run the argument. The Russians re-gilded the domes of Orthodox churches, despite being officially an atheist state. We no longer believe in gods, but for centuries we did and isn't that part of our history? And they were rather fine buildings, weren't they? Christian Britain didn't demolish Stonehenge because it was constructed by bygone pagans. This is in marked contrast to the Taliban in Afghanistan who deliberately blew up the Buddhas at Bamyan simply because they were built by non-Muslims – even though in so doing they were destroying a part of their country's history.

The object of our visit to Belgium was to visit the European Parliament, at the invitation of our MEP. Annie had made all the

The Cloth Hall

arrangements, as it was her idea in the first place. She knew MEPs could be approached to host visits by constituents, and wanted us to take advantage of this so as to be able to see the Parliament in session. What struck me was how unhurried and relaxed the atmosphere was in the debating chamber – very businesslike, speakers addressing the assembly in a variety of languages and no one waving papers in the air, shouting 'Hear! Hear!' or braying abuse as they do in our House of Commons or indeed showing much emotion at all.

We travelled by coach via Calais, stopped for lunch where Annie had booked us in and then on arrival at our hotel in Brussels found that two of our number had formerly lived and worked in the city so knew where to locate suitable restaurants for dinner. We negotiated a price for 28 of us, and were given wine 'on the house'. My most vivid memory of the city is of how the *Grand Place* more than lived up to its reputation when I saw it for real.

On the return journey we had planned to visit one of the many First World War cemeteries dotted all over Flanders. We had travelled to the European Parliament as an official delegation representing Romsey Liberal Democrats, and it had been agreed that as chairman I would formally lay a wreath on behalf of the Association. The day was a bright and sunny, but during the night it had been snowing. We were the first visitors to the cemetery that morning and it looked wonderfully serene and peaceful with its pristine covering of glistening white snow unblemished by footprints. The contrast now with what it must have been like in 1915 challenged the imagination.

I'm sure Ieper will repay a longer visit, if only to see if the restaurant we popped into on the street corner is still featuring a dish with includes sea urchin caviar. I'd been joined by my friend Carol, both looking for a snack in what looked like a bar. We thought it was merely a bar which also served food, but when we got inside and were conducted to a table by a waiter it was too late to turn back without embarrassment. It was, in fact, a top class establishment with excellent service and amazing food – including the afore-mentioned sea urchin caviar. I didn't know sea urchins *had* caviar – and I'm pretty sure sea urchins don't know it, either. But we ordered it just to see what it was. I'm none the wiser. It was there on the plate, somewhere. I just couldn't find it. The fish was beautifully cooked and served. The accompanying scallops white, fleshy and round. Maybe the 'caviar' was in the sauce. Preceded by an *amuse-bouche* of salmon mousse served up on a biscuit and garnished with what looked like horsehair and which was delivered to our table without being ordered – it was that sort of restaurant. I might go back to Ieper just to sit again at that same table and give myself the time to tackle their *gourmet* menu. Now there's a thought! Or I'll go back to see the rest of the town and do a bit of shopping, see the inside of the Cloth Hall, and then 'do' the Menin Gate just like all the other tourists.

January 2004

POSTSCRIPT
Q: If the King were to officiate at the opening of a brothel, how would his arrival be announced?
A: With a fanfare of strumpets.

Goodnight.

Z

ZAGORSK*

If the opposite of 'uncouth' is 'couth', so the opposite of 'out of kilter' must be 'in'.

In the immediate postwar period a World Festival of Youth and Students was held in alternate years in Communist bloc capitals, and having spent half my national service studying Russian naturally I strained every sinew and knifed every piggy bank to come up with the money when it was Moscow's turn to play host. Like anyone who's studied a foreign language I wanted the chance to speak it with people for whom it was their mother tongue, and confirm that what I'd spent so much time and effort learning actually worked.

In those days it was nigh on impossible to get across the Iron Curtain into Eastern Europe or the Soviet Union unless you had a personal invitation from a local, were a member of some or other official delegation or were a member of your own country's Communist Party. But this was just a year after the Hungarian uprising and the Soviets were desperate to entice as many young people from the West as possible to take part in the festival, hoping for the propaganda benefits of drawing a veil over what they'd done in Budapest. By bragging about the numbers coming they could claim that our presence in Moscow showed our support for the Soviet Union and its policies.

Joining the special train in London, I fell in with a group of Scots. They seemed fascinated by my strange accent – mutual, I wasn't used to broad Glaswegian. But we stuck together throughout the long journey, turning our compartment into a fortress and keeping everyone else out. To improve personal comfort we put all our baggage on the floor, so as to provide a level space between the two banks of seats and support under the knees if you put your legs out straight. With the luggage rack therefore empty we could take it in turns to climb up and crash out full length and get some proper sleep. When the journey is going to take three days without getting off the train, such considerations are important. In Berlin food parcels were handed out. It was the first time I'd ever come across pumpernickel; I wasn't sure whether to eat it or mend the holes in my shoes. As we were crossing the interminable North European Plain through Poland – nothing to see but unchanging fields and woods, and you look through the window an hour later and it's as though you haven't moved – a farm worker in a field saw our train passing and made a dismissive gesture. So much for solidarity with the people. At each station we stopped at there was a welcoming party to wave flags and hand out refreshment. Even at Minsk, where we arrived at two in the morning. All volunteers, of course. Of *course* – and my other leg plays '*Rule Britannia*'.

Our hostel was on the outskirts of Moscow and we were fed communally, in cavernous marquees set out to seat hundreds. There were some fifty thousand young people attending the festival, with nationalities all mixed up. Meals were self-service. Our choice of breakfast food was laid out on long tables, and included both red and black caviar. This led to one chap queueing alongside me choosing some red, spreading it on a chunk of bread and then remarking to me 'This strawberry jam tastes fishy.' A bonus was that we were quite near the Vystavka, a permanent exhibition of life in each of the Soviet Union's constituent republics and autonomous areas. I went several times, and learned a lot. The staff in each republic's pavilion wore traditional costume and had products from their homeland laid out for inspection.

They all spoke Russian in addition to their regional language and were there to answer questions. It was the sort of 'live exhibit' that schoolchildren doing projects dream of. For us from the UK part of the attraction was that some of the regions were totally unknown to us – we'd never even heard of them and had absolutely no idea where they were. If you were given a map of Russia, could *you* indicate exactly where Tuva is or where to find the Evenki? Most British people wouldn't know whether Evenki is a place, a people, a small mammal, a wild flower or a sexually transmitted disease of reindeer (*'Sorry, Santa. Rudolph can't pull your sleigh tonight – he's got a touch of the evenks.'*). Let alone where it's spoken (*clue!*).

My new Scots friend Jock (yes – really!) had brought his kilt, and for some reason a spare one. I tried it on just for fun, but discovering

The pavilion of the Turkmen republic

and the Karelo-Finnish republic

that in fact it was very comfortable I then wore it for the rest of our stay. Jock and I went round together as a lark to confuse the members of the other delegations who became totally bemused when on greeting me with the Russian word for a Scotsman – *'shotlandyets'* – I immediately riposted – *'Nyet, anglichanin.'* 'The English wear kilts too?' 'No. Only me'. I dare say there exist family photograph albums in obscure parts of the world with pictures of two Scotsmen in national dress taken by granddad when he went to Moscow fifty years ago – only one of them said he was an Englishman. Huh? So was that an expression of cultural diversity? No. Just the English sense of humour.

In Gorki Park the city fathers had laid out paved areas for devotees of a wide range of activities: easels for artists, squares for chess players, tables for practitioners of table tennis, benches for string players and so on and so on. Whatever your hobby, if you wanted to spend time with others who shared your interest then in your free time you could go to Gorki Park to 'your' open-air space and meet other likeminded people. I was watching chess games when a group of amateur sculptors accosted me and insisted that I pose for them. I didn't kid myself that this was because of my personal pulchritude, universally admired though that has always been. It was because I had a beard. In those days that was so unusual that they'd probably never seen a real one and wanted the challenge of trying to model it in clay.

Within the walls of the Kremlin lie several cathedrals dating from the fifteenth century, and adjacent stands St Basil's. Elsewhere in the city, however, little remains of pre-nineteenth century Moscow. This is partly because the medieval town outside the fortified area (the 'kremlin') was built of wood and so unlikely to survive, especially considering the local climate. A second reason is that when Napoleon occupied the city in 1812 the inhabitants themselves set fire to it as winter approached in order to deny the invaders shelter and increase the pressure on them to abandon the occupation and go. To see more examples of medieval Russian ecclesiastical construction I would have to leave the city and travel to what tourist brochures nowadays heavily promote as 'The Golden Ring', north-east of Moscow.

My enquiries about making such a visit evoked a firmly negative response: participants in the Festival were not permitted to leave Moscow independently. I decided to see if this was really the case. The nearest town on the 'Ring' circuit, Zagorsk, was only some

50kms distant, so why not try just to get that far? If I turned up at the railway station and asked for a ticket, would I get one? Only one way to find out. It worked – no problem! Jock and I just got on the train, visited the Trinity Lavra monastery and got a train back. No one questioned us, and even though I was speaking Russian we weren't going to pass as natives when dressed in clothes obviously not 'Made in the Soviet Union' (and no – we ditched the kilts on this occasion. There is such a thing as pushing your luck!).

The Trinity Lavra monastery

There was a wide variety of organised visits and excursions on offer, and one I took was to the Valdai Hills some 350km north-west of Moscow. It was an opportunity – even rarer in those days than the chance to visit a Russian city – to see what rural Russia looked like. One of the local guides accompanying us made a lasting impression: by name Yefim ('Fima' in familiar Russian), he absolutely insisted on taking my rucksack off me and carrying it himself, even though it had only my jumper and a pocket dictionary in it and weighed practically nothing. I guess he was under instructions to make things as easy as possible for the visitors, but to take it to such an extreme was nonsensical. I protested, but he just refused to budge and I gave way to avoid embarrassing the rest of our party and maybe getting him into trouble with the authorities. But I didn't *forget* – as is demonstrated by the fact that although it's almost sixty years ago here I am telling you about it! *(And I still remember his surname, too – but won't reveal it in case he's still alive and would be embarrassed to have the incident recalled).*

In the Valdai Hills: Lake Seliger, near Ostashkov

Free tickets for performances at the Bolshoi Theatre were handed out at reception at our hostel, and I drew *Evgeny Onegin*. It was a wonderful surprise to see the inside of the theatre, knowing how much else of historic beauty and luxury the Russians had deliberately destroyed during the Revolution. We were taken on guided tours of the Kremlin, where for the first time I came face to face – literally – with Orthodox iconography (you can read more about that under 'N' – but in the *Little Green Nightbook*, not this one). The deepest impression was attending a service in the cathedral, because Orthodox ritual was so totally unlike what I was used to back home in my Anglican church choir. We were given places of honour at the side of what in an English church would be called the chancel, and we could hear the choir of three hundred singing behind the screen out of sight of us and the congregation. Except they weren't three hundred, just twelve. Then the archimandrite walked past us to the chancel steps, singing a rich bass *fortissimo*. As he passed me, and without any change in his facial expression, he doubled the volume! Reaching the steps, he raised his hand. The congregation, who had been standing in complete silence for nearly an hour, were awaiting this signal. He dropped his hand and they all started singing and continued for twenty minutes non-stop – all without hymn books, psalteries or anything whatever, all entirely from memory. Then the Patriarch came to the pulpit to preach his sermon, taking as his theme 'love'. He absolutely looked the part: long grey beard, very pale skin, piercing blue eyes and benign expression, and wearing a gold tiara topped by a cross and the sumptuous vestments that went with his rank. All familiar enough to most of us nowadays from television, but overwhelming to experience it for real in the Kremlin in the heart of Moscow when Russia was still the Soviet Union and officially an atheist state...

I said it left an abiding memory. After the service the Patriarch distributed tiny golden souvenir crosses to his Western guests.

I still treasure mine.

*Zagorsk, so named by the Communists in 1930 after the revolutionary activist Vladimir Zagorsky, reverted in 1991 to its original medieval name of Sergiyev Posad, which honoured its close connection with St Sergius of Radonezh, a Russian monk who in the fourteenth century founded some 40 monasteries.

In September 2012 I visited again, in the company of my friend Mike whom you read about hitchhiking with me around Norway, and with me again (fifty-three years later!) in Ulan Bator taking photos. Sergiev Posad is the official residence of the Patriarch of the Russian Orthodox Church, and the monastic compound was seething with tourists and all approaches lined with stalls selling souvenirs of every description. It was Sunday, and by chance also the beginning of 'term' for new seminarians, who were all gathered on the steps of the cathedral for a group photo under the gaze of proud parents and other family members (also taking photos).

August 1957

POSTSCRIPT
Our local garden centre has closed down. The customers stopped coming and it had no fuchsia.

Goodnight.

EPILOGUE
TO MARGARET
And her eyes were of the sea, my lads,
And her eyes were of the sea.
And the blue of the far, far distant blue
Of horizons lost in the sun-dipped blue
Of the sea on a solent summer's day.
With a yacht sail thwart of a breeze o' the west
And a wafting gull and a wisp of my hair
And Beaulieu's creek and a tramper's smoke
And her eyes were of the sea, my lads,
And her eyes were of the sea.

On Lepe's mere strand and the distant isle
Which lead a-down to the needling crag
And the great full-riggers which once on a day
Proudly the name of England bore
To the lands which are far away.
And a tricorn hat and Elizabeth's men,
The walls of Southampton standing alert,
And Sally-port of Portsmouth old,
The Nab Tower's brood like chessmen placed
And the yachts of Cowes and Hamble a-port
Of this shade of a tree on the Solent shore
And her eyes were of the sea, my lads,
And her eyes were of the sea.

A shot in the arm and drug to my soul
Is the blue of the far, far distant blue
And the sun a-glinting the Solent's crests.
The toil of the world can pass me by
With its struggle of power and such worthless things
And its claim to dictate who is friend or foe
And where I may go and what believe
Be it mausoleum by Kremlin wall
Or he who died on Calvary.
For when these are forgotten and Man gone too
Who will remain with none to view
The blue of the far, far distant blue
Of horizons lost in the sun-dipped blue
Of the sea on a solent summer's day?
And the eyes that are of the sea, my lads,
And the eyes that are of the sea.

21 August 1957
Frankfurt a/Main

Between 1944 and 1968 the Students' Union at Southampton University published a literary magazine, *Second Wessex*. This poem appeared in the Spring 1958 edition.

ACKNOWLEDGMENTS

The author wishes to express his thanks to:

My one-time next door neighbour Derek Snowdon, an established artist, for his creativity in many of the stories in providing amusing illustrations.

My long-standing friend Carol Boulton, proprietor of Russell Stables in West End, Southampton, and mastermind behind the Epona Trust, for reading initial drafts of these stories and suggesting adjustments.

My oldest friend, Mike Roberts, whose recollections of hitchhiking with me in Norway in 1959 helped shamfer the edges of those particular stories, and whose photos taken when we travelled to Mongolia in 2012 provided complementary visual material.

To Judith Blake, on behalf of Sarsen Press, for her forbearance in patiently accepting the frequent amendments over many months to which my original drafts were subjected in order to produce the final result.